make your own
farm animals
and more

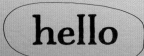
hello

make your own farm animals
and more

your own

35 projects for kids using everyday cardboard packaging

Tracey Radford

CICO BOOKS
LONDON NEW YORK

To Tim, for his enthusiasm and support,
and for putting up with all the cardboard!

Published in 2017 by CICO Books

An imprint of Ryland Peters & Small Ltd

20–21 Jockey's Fields   341 E 116th St
London WC1R 4BW   New York, NY 10029

www.rylandpeters.com

10 9 8 7 6 5 4 3 2 1

A CIP catalog record for this book is available from the Library of
Congress and the British Library.

ISBN: 978 1 78249 421 8

Printed in China

Editor: Katie Hardwicke
Designer: Emily Breen
Photographer: Martin Norris
Template illustrations: Stephen Dew

In-house editor: Dawn Bates
Art director: Sally Powell
Production controller: Mai-ling Collyer
Publishing manager: Penny Craig
Publisher: Cindy Richards

A note about measurements: All the measurements are given in
both imperial and metric, but the conversions have sometimes
been adjusted for the sake of the project.

Contents

Introduction

In many ways a farm was an obvious choice for my second craft book, seeing as we live next door to one, so I didn't have to go far for inspiration! In fact, many of the projects were thought up as I trudged along the lanes near our house, past fields of grazing cows and flocks of sheep.

The main ideas at the heart of the book are the same as those for my first book, *Make Your Own Zoo*—namely that it's themed, uses inexpensive, easy-to-get-hold-of materials like cardboard tubes and egg cartons, and that the projects are roughly in proportion and all work together, so you can keep adding to your farm to make it the way you want it to be. As well as transforming very ordinary stuff, this is craft you can play with!

The farm animals soon come to life with a little cutting, gluing, and painting. You'll find that a lot of the techniques are repeated, so that once you've mastered a cow for example, it's very easy to make the horse or bull to join her in the field. Half the fun of the projects is putting them all together in a farmyard setting, so I've included buildings, machinery, and scenery to make everyone feel at home, along with Fred the Farmer and his wife, Winnie, to keep things running smoothly. Working with cardboard packaging isn't an exact science—sizes, shapes, and colors vary. I've tried to accommodate this as best as I can, but don't be afraid to adapt the projects to suit you, and what you've got to work with.

It's also possible to adapt and simplify projects for younger children—this is something I've been doing at my *Make Your Own Zoo* workshops, where I craft with kids of all ages. There are a few suggestions in the book for modifying the projects, but I'm sure you'll come up with your own ideas, too. I've seen some wonderful, colorful, crazy animals at the workshops—and that really is what it's all about, encouraging creativity and imagination.

So, cardboard ready? Let's get making!

SAFETY MATTERS

The projects in this book are for you and your child to do together and are suitable for children approximately six years and older. Always keep a close eye on children while you are helping them and never leave children alone with scissors or glue, even for a few minutes.

Tools & Materials

You should find most of what you need to construct the projects around the house—but, before you get going, here's a list of a few essentials to keep in your craft corner, plus some handy tips and techniques to help things go smoothly.

Scissors

There's plenty of scissor practice in this book! Cutting is a key part of most of the projects and should always be supervised. Sometimes it'll be challenging, like learning to pierce holes, cut slots, or snip out small shapes, but practice really does make perfect. This book is for children aged six and over—having said that, scissor skills vary at all ages. You are the best judge of how much help to give your child, but bear in mind, the more cutting you let them do, the better their scissor skills will be.

As well as a good pair of kids' craft scissors—called craft scissors in the projects—you'll need large scissors (with long blades), and some small, sharp ones; these are important in several projects. Straight-edged nail scissors are ideal, because they're sharp enough to make holes for slots. When a project specifies small scissors, these are the ones you'll need. Embroidery or needlework scissors work well, too.

The best technique I've found to help children use these small scissors safely to make holes, is to keep the scissors closed and press down firmly on the cardboard, twisting slightly from side to side until the tip pierces through. You might find putting a ball of modeling clay (Plasticine) behind the cardboard helps, as it gives something to push against.

When a particular type of scissors is not specified, use whichever size you feel most comfortable with.

Glue

The best glue to use is craft (PVA) glue, which is widely available. It's washable and easy to paint over. The problem sometimes is it can be quite runny, so glued-on pieces may slip. A top tip to get around this is to make tacky glue. Pour a small amount of craft (PVA) glue—no more than ½ in. (1 cm)—into an old, clean jar or yogurt pot. Leave, uncovered, somewhere out of reach. After about a day, it should start thickening up—this will happen more quickly in warm conditions. The longer you leave it, the tackier it gets. In the instructions, this is what tacky glue refers to. Keep an eye on it, and either top up as you use it, or have a few containers on the go. Once it's the right consistency, cover it, to stop the glue setting. Tacky glue is especially useful for the tractor project (see page 99).

A glue stick is very handy for sticking down paper, so it doesn't get too wet and crinkly— for example, covering the trailer or gluing grass around the pond. When it comes to gluing card to a cork, a stronger, all-purpose, clear adhesive works best.

Paint

Ready-mixed kids' poster or acrylic paints are what you need. Tempera-based paints are good too. All the colors to paint the animals can be made from red, yellow, blue, white, and black. Usually a pack of six paints will include a nice bright green as well.

Paintbrushes

A decent selection of different-sized brushes helps. Small, fine brushes are good for things like painting birds or adding detail to some of the animals' faces and bodies. Bigger brushes are ideal for speeding up scenery painting. A great tip is to use a bristle pastry brush! They're soft and flexible and wonderful for painting bigger pieces of cereal-box card or cardboard tubes.

Pens

A good fine black felt-tip pen or gel pen is great for adding detail to faces. Use whichever one you prefer, or have at home. Some of the projects also call for a black permanent marker pen with a fine or medium nib, like a Sharpie. This is because they don't rub off shiny cereal-box card and make light work of coloring in over paint, like the tractor or trailer wheels on page 106.

Cardboard tubes

Toilet-paper tubes are especially useful, but gather up a few paper-towel (kitchen paper) tubes and giftwrap tubes too. Make sure you have a good mix of different tube widths.

Egg cartons

Not all egg cartons are exactly alike. Some are better for cutting out a good egg-cup shape (the molded piece that holds the egg) and others might be better for cones (the pointy cardboard pieces in the middle of a carton that protect the eggs). You'll find some egg-cup pieces are squarer on the bottom, or have shorter sides, while some cones are larger or less pointy than others. Some cartons don't have cones at all. If your carton has cones with holes in the top and you want to make a bird or rabbit, brush glue inside the top part of the cone, and push a small scrunched-up piece of newspaper into the glue, to block the hole.

Please don't worry if your animals look a little different to the ones here—this is the nature of this kind of craft, when materials vary; have fun making the most of what you've got and tweaking here and there if you need to, to make your own unique creations. It's not just the egg cups and cones that are useful—

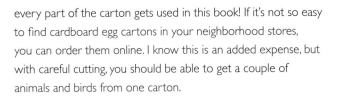

RECYCLING

Every element of the farm is made from either cardboard tubes, egg cartons, or cereal boxes—or all three, and some use other packaging, such as corks or yogurt pots, that is easy to source. It pays to have a good collection of recyclables because they vary in size and shape.

every part of the carton gets used in this book! If it's not so easy to find cardboard egg cartons in your neighborhood stores, you can order them online. I know this is an added expense, but with careful cutting, you should be able to get a couple of animals and birds from one carton.

Cereal-box cardboard

This is another kids' craft staple. The only drawback is that the shiny side is often difficult to paint. I got round this problem in some of the larger projects by turning the box inside out. If you want to paint both sides, rub the shiny side with sandpaper to remove the sheen and help the paint to grip to the surface. You may need to apply a few coats. Adding white paint to the color mix usually helps improve coverage, too. I often use cardboard from an egg carton lid instead of cereal-box cardboard, especially for the smaller creatures. This is because it's usually easier to paint both sides. Pull off any labels first.

in the field

Take a walk through the fields and see who's there,
but if the bull's about, you'd better beware!

Sneaky Sheep

The sheep are always breaking out, it drives the farmer mad. He's often mending fences, but they're good at being baa-d!

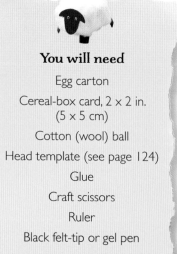

You will need

Egg carton

Cereal-box card, 2 x 2 in.
(5 x 5 cm)

Cotton (wool) ball

Head template (see page 124)

Glue

Craft scissors

Ruler

Black felt-tip or gel pen

1 Cut an egg cup from the carton and straighten the edge so it sits flat and the cup is about ¾ in. (2 cm) high. Don't worry if there are a few gaps in the sides from the carton joins (like the one in the picture)—this won't affect your sheep!

2 For the legs, use the black pen to draw two small black squares on opposite sides of the cup (avoiding any gaps), right on the edge. Then draw two more, halfway between the first ones, so you end up with four evenly spaced legs around the cup. Color-in the squares and try to make them the same size.

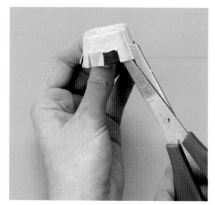

3 Snip up the sides of the marked legs and also snip the card halfway between each leg.

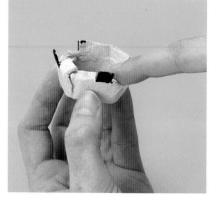

4 Now push these flaps of card up into the cup (under the body), leaving the legs down.

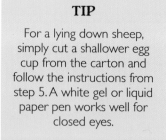

TIP

For a lying down sheep, simply cut a shallower egg cup from the carton and follow the instructions from step 5. A white gel or liquid paper pen works well for closed eyes.

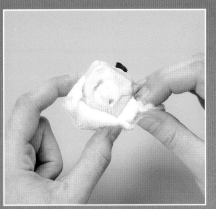

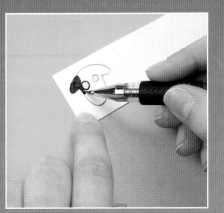

5 Cover the top of your sheep's body with a good layer of glue. Tease out a small piece of cotton ball so it's not too thick, then start pressing it into the glue. Begin around the bottom edge, just above the legs, and work round, finishing on top. A thin coat of cotton ball looks best.

6 While the glue is drying, copy the head template onto some cereal-box card. Draw circles where you want the eyes to be, and color around them with the black pen. Add a tiny dot inside the eyes.

7 Carefully cut out the head and glue it onto the body. You could add a little tuft of cotton ball between the ears, if you want.

baa

baa

Ruby Rabbit

Hoppity, hoppity, hoppity hop, but where's she hopping to?
Ruby's quite forgetful and hasn't got a clue!

You will need

Egg carton

Ears template (see page 125)

Cotton (wool) ball

Paints in colors of your choice
for rabbit fur, and white and red

Fine paintbrush

Glue (tacky glue is best,
see page 8)

Craft scissors

Small scissors (see page 8)
(optional)

Ruler

Pencil

Fine black felt-tip or gel pen

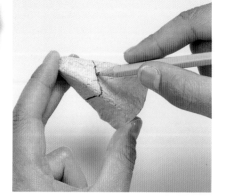

1 Roughly cut a whole cone from the egg carton. Use a pencil and ruler to mark 1¼ in. (3 cm) down from the top on one side and draw a line across. Draw another line on the opposite side, ¾ in. (2 cm) from the top. Join them with sloping lines either side.

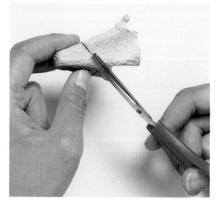

2 To cut out the body, snip up two adjacent corners to the pencil line, fold the flap back, and cut it off—it's now easier to cut along the rest of the line.

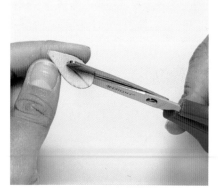

3 Copy the ears template on page 125 onto a piece of the egg carton lid and cut out the teardrop shape. Then draw on the ears using the dotted lines on the template as a guide, and snip out the small piece of card between them.

4 There are two options for attaching the ears. The first (and easiest) is to brush glue on the bottom part of the ears and stick them just behind the top of the cone (on the longer side). When dry, bend the ears back slightly. Go to step 6.

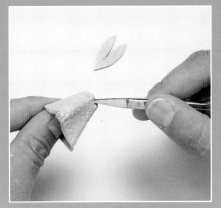

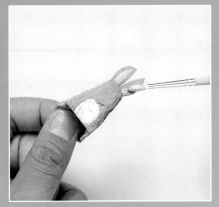

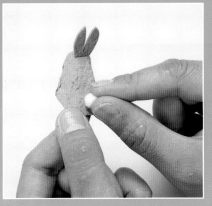

5 Or, you can make a slot for the ears. Use the small scissors to pierce a hole just behind the top of the cone, on the longer side—keep the scissors closed, press down carefully, and twist gently from side to side to make a hole. Snip the slot to make it wide enough to fit the bottom part of the ears. Dab some glue inside the cone behind the slot, and push the ears into place.

6 When the glue is dry, paint your rabbit any color you like, remembering to paint both sides of the ears. When touch dry, use a fine paintbrush to add a white fluffy chest. Mix pink from red and white, and paint a line inside each ear.

7 For the tail, pull off a tiny piece of cotton ball and roll it into a little ball between your finger and thumb. Glue it to the back of the body near the base.

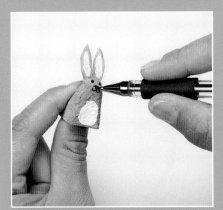

8 When the paint is dry, use the fine black pen to draw eyes below the ears and a twitchy nose right on the edge of the cone top.

True Blue

True Blue jumps like a dream over fences and water,
and he's loved to bits by the farmer's daughter.

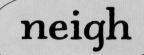

You will need

2 toilet-paper tubes or a kitchen-paper tube (narrow ones are best)

Cereal-box card, 5 × 5 in (12 × 12 cm)

Head and tail templates (see page 125)

Sheet of newspaper

Black and white paint

Paintbrush

Craft scissors

Small scissors (see page 8)

Ruler

Pencil

Fine black felt-tip or gel pen

1 Start with the legs. Take one of the cardboard tubes and flatten it with your hand. Cut along the creases so you have two pieces of card. Take one piece and fold it in half lengthwise, pressing the crease. Cut along the crease to make two strips, each about 1¼ in. (3 cm) wide—if they are a lot wider, trim to size.

2 Carefully fold each strip in half lengthwise again, pressing down firmly to hold the crease in place. These are the legs.

3 Use the other toilet-paper tube to make the body, it needs to be about 3 in. (8 cm) long. Measure 3 in. (8 cm) from the top of the tube and mark with a pencil. Squeeze the sides together near the mark, and cut across the tube.

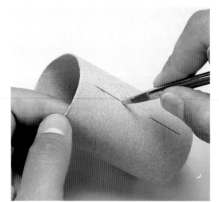

4 To make slots for the legs, hold a ruler along the length of the tube and use a pencil to draw two lines, both ¾ in. (2 cm) long, about ¼ in. (1 cm) in from each end. Repeat this 1 in. (3 cm) farther around the tube, so the leg slots line up.

5 Keeping the small scissors closed, place the point at one end of one of the lines and press down, carefully twisting the scissors back and forth. Once you've made a hole, cut along the line. Repeat for the other slots, making sure they are big enough for the leg pieces.

6 Wiggle a pair of closed craft scissors in and out of the slots to help open them up, then thread the leg pieces through. When they're level, firmly fold the legs inward, making sure the crease is as close to the slots as possible.

neigh

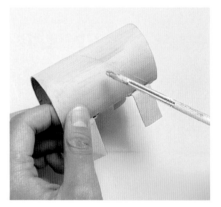

7 Trim the legs until you're happy with the length, and the body stands steady and level.

8 Mix a gray from black and white paint, and paint the body and legs. When the paint isn't too wet, leave the body on its back or side to finish drying, so the legs don't do the splits! Bend them firmly back into place once the paint is completely dry.

18 in the field

9 While the body is drying, copy the head and tail templates on page 125 onto the piece of cereal-box card and cut them out.

10 Paint the head and tail in gray and then add the mane and tail hair in white (remember to add the forelock between the ears). True Blue has a few dappled spots near the back of his body, so add some now if you'd like to, then draw on the eyes and nostrils with a black pen, adding a line to define the head.

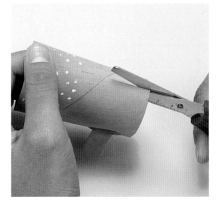

11 When the paint is dry, cut a slot for the head piece at one end of the body, checking that it is the right length—the head should slide in all the way to the front of the neck. If the mane sits too far above the slot, trim the bottom of the head piece. Some of True Blue's chest should stick out of the tube.

12 Scrunch up two small pieces of newspaper and push them into the tube, either side of True Blue's chest, to keep the head steady.

13 Cut a short slot at the other end for the tail. Only part of the tail needs to slot in, and the top should sit a little above the body to give it a jaunty swish.

TIP

If you prefer, paint a chestnut horse by mixing red and yellow paint with a dab of blue to make brown.

Clarissa the Cow

Clarissa likes to take her time while finding grass to munch, as soon as she's had breakfast, it's almost time for lunch!

You will need

Egg carton

2 toilet-paper tubes (or a kitchen-paper tube)

Sheet of newspaper

White, black, and red paint

Fine paintbrush

Big paintbrush

Glue (tacky glue is best, see page 8)

Craft scissors

Small scissors (see page 8)

Ruler

Pencil

Fine black felt-tip or gel pen

Black marker pen with a fine/medium nib (optional)

1 Cut the head from the molded part inside the end of an egg carton. Draw lines each side of the raised section for the muzzle. Draw ears sticking out to the sides—the top of each ear reaches the base of an egg cup—then follow the curves up to the join. Don't worry about the lumpy card join between the cups.

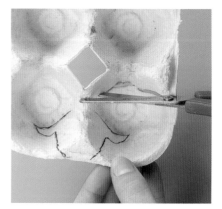

2 Roughly cut out the cow's head shape, making sure you keep as much of the card join between the ears as possible.

3 Neaten up and carefully snip the card join to gently round off the top of the head. If you can, leave a little of the rough edge from the join for a forelock—this adds a bit of character.

moo

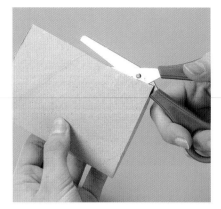

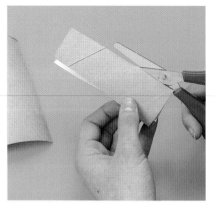

4 For the legs, take one of the toilet-paper tubes and flatten it with your hand. Cut along the creases so you have two pieces of card. Keep one for later on in the project.

5 Take the other piece of card and fold it in half lengthwise, pressing the crease. Cut along the crease to make two strips, each about 1¼ in. (3 cm) wide—if they are a lot wider, trim to size. Carefully fold each strip in half lengthwise again, pressing down firmly to hold the crease in place. These are the legs.

6 Use the other toilet-paper tube to make the body—it needs to be about 3 in. (8 cm) long. Measure 3 in. (8 cm) from the top of the tube and mark with a pencil. Squeeze the sides together near the mark, and cut across the tube.

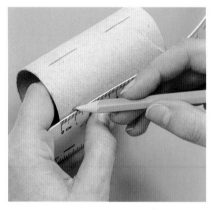

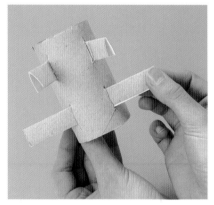

7 To make slots for the legs, hold a ruler along the length of the tube and use a pencil to draw two lines, both ¾ in. (2 cm) long, about ¼ in. (1 cm) in from each end. Repeat this 1 in. (3 cm) farther around the tube, so the leg slots line up.

8 Keeping the small scissors closed, place the point at one end of one of the lines and press down, carefully twisting the scissors back and forth. Once you've made a hole, cut along the line. Repeat for the other slots, making sure they are big enough for the leg pieces.

9 Wiggle a pair of closed craft scissors in and out of the slots to help open them up, then thread the leg pieces through. When they're level, firmly fold the legs inward, making sure the crease is as close to the slots as possible.

10 Trim the legs until you're happy with the length, and the body stands steady and level.

11 For the cow's neck, cut a piece of newspaper about 8 × 8 in. (20 × 20 cm), loosely fold the edges into the middle, then scrunch it up into a loose ball. Brush glue inside one end of the body tube and push the ball of newspaper in, making sure a little sticks out the end.

12 Glue the head onto the newspaper, with the top of the head close to the top edge of the tube. Cut a thin strip for a tail, using card leftover from making the legs. Make the tail longer than you want it to be, and stick the extra part inside the tube end.

13 Once the glue is dry, paint your whole cow white. When the paint isn't too wet, leave the body on its back or side to finish drying, so the legs don't do the splits! Bend them firmly back into place when the paint is completely dry.

14 Paint the black markings on the body and tail. With a black felt-tip pen, draw circles to outline where you want the eyes to be, then paint around them with a fine brush, or use a black marker pen to add markings to the head.

15 Paint or color in a pink snout and, when dry, draw on nostrils with the fine black pen.

16 Push a piece of scrunched-up newspaper in at the tail end to help your cow balance. Hold the tail where it joins the body and bend it down into place over the end.

Bobbie the Bull

**Bobbie is a football fan, he'd really love to play,
but when he tries to kick a ball his hooves get in the way.**

You will need

Egg carton

2 toilet-paper tubes

Sheet of newspaper

Kitchen foil

Horn template (see page 125)

Red, yellow, blue, and white paint

Fine paintbrush

Big paintbrush

Craft scissors

Small scissors (see page 8)

Glue (tacky glue is best, see page 8)

Paper clips (optional)

Ruler

Pencil

Fine black felt-tip or gel pen

1 The head is cut from the molded part inside the end of an egg carton. Draw lines either side of the raised section for the muzzle. Draw ears sticking out to the sides—the top of each ear should reach the base of an egg cup—then follow the egg cup curves up to the join. Don't worry about the lumpy card join between the cups.

2 Roughly cut out your head shape, making sure you keep as much of the card join between the ears as possible. Neaten up, and carefully snip the card join to gently round off the top of the head. If you can, leave a little of the rough edge from the join for a forelock—this adds a bit of character.

3 For the legs, take one of the toilet-paper tubes and flatten it with your hand. Cut along the creases so you have two pieces of card. Keep one for later on in the project.

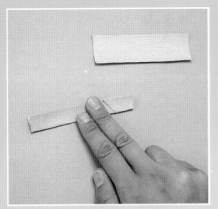

4 Take the other piece of card and fold it in half lengthwise. Cut along this crease. Each strip should be about 1¼ in. (3 cm) wide—if they are a lot wider, trim to size. Carefully fold each strip in half lengthwise again, pressing down firmly to hold the crease in place. These are the legs.

5 Use the other tube to make the body, it needs to be about 3 in. (8 cm) long. Measure 3 in. (8 cm) from the top of the tube and mark with a pencil. Squeeze the end of the tube near the mark, and cut across the tube.

6 To make slots for the legs, hold a ruler along the length of the tube and use a pencil to draw two lines, both ¾ in. (2 cm) long, about ¼ in. (1 cm) in from each end. Repeat this 1 in. (3 cm) farther around the tube, so the leg slots line up.

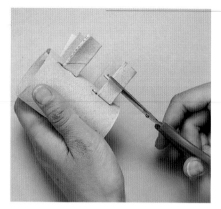

7 Keeping the small scissors closed, place the point at one end of one of the lines and press down, carefully twisting the scissors back and forth. Once you've made a hole, cut along the line. Repeat for the other slots, making sure they are big enough for the leg pieces.

8 Wiggle a pair of closed craft scissors in and out of the slots to open them up, then thread the leg pieces through.

9 When they're level, firmly fold the legs inward, making sure the crease is as close to the slots as possible. Trim the legs until you're happy with the length, and the body stands steady and level.

10 For the bull's neck, cut a piece of newspaper about 8 x 8 in. (20 x 20 cm), loosely fold the edges into the middle, then scrunch it up into a loose ball.

11 Brush glue inside one end of the body tube and push the ball of newspaper in, making sure a little sticks out the end. Cut a thin strip for a tail, using card leftover from making the legs. Make the tail longer than you want it to be, and stick the extra part inside the tube end.

12 When the glue is dry, mix a rich brown color (mix red, yellow and a little blue) and paint the body, tail, and legs, painting the newspaper, too. Paint the head, adding a little white to the brown to make the snout lighter. When the paint isn't too wet, leave the body on its back or side to finish drying, so the legs don't do the splits! Bend them firmly back into place when the paint is dry.

13 Copy the template on page 125 and cut out two bull's horns from leftover card. Glue the horns behind the head, lining them up with the edge between the ears. Use paper clips to hold them in place if needed.

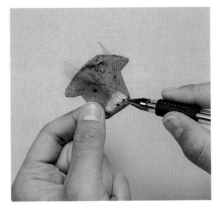

14 Draw on the eyes and nostrils with the fine black pen.

15 Carefully roll a small piece of kitchen foil, about 1 x 1 in. (3 x 3 cm), as tightly as you can. It's a little fiddly, but once started, you can roll it between your thumb and finger to make a thin, bendy stick.

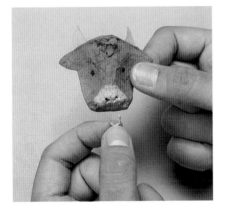

16 Bend part of the foil roll into a half-ring shape to fit between the bull's nostrils, trim it to size, then glue in place.

17 Now glue Bobbie's head onto the painted newspaper, with the top of the head close to the top edge of the tube.

18 Scrunch up another piece of newspaper and push it in the tail end to help Bobbie to balance. Hold the tail where it joins the body and bend it down, into place.

Bluebird and Robin

Bluebird and Robin are Superhero mad, and dream of fighting villains from their secret tree-top pad.

You will need

Egg carton

Templates on page 125

Craft scissors

Small scissors (see page 8) (optional)

Glue (tacky glue is best, see page 8)

Blue, red, yellow, and white paint

Fine paintbrush

Ruler

Pencil

Fine black felt-tip or gel pen

Thin strip of cereal box card (optional)

Yellow felt-tip pen (optional)

1 To make the body, roughly cut out a whole cone from the egg carton, so it's easier to work with. Cut one for each bird. Use a pencil to mark ¾ in. (2 cm) down from the top on all sides and join the marks with a line.

2 Snip up all four corners to the line. Bend back the four flaps. Cut three of them off, leaving one flap still attached for the tail feathers. Trim this to about ½ in. (1 cm) long.

3 On the remaining flap, snip off the corners at an angle to make a "V," or you could draw a "V" first with a pencil and cut along the lines. Bend the tail feathers back so they sit flat.

4 Copy the templates on page 125 and cut out two wings and the extra tail feather part from the egg carton lid or a piece of spare card.

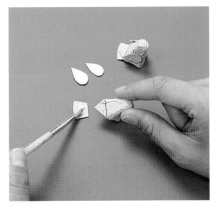

5 Apply a little glue to the wings and stick them either side of the body. Glue the extra tail feather piece to the underside of the "V".

6 When the glue is dry, paint Bluebird pale blue and Robin light brown. You can mix a brown from yellow and red with a dab of blue, then lighten it with some white to get the perfect shade. When Robin is touch dry, use a fine paintbrush to paint his tummy and face red.

7 When the paint is dry, use a fine black pen to dot eyes near the very top of the cone. Keep them small and quite close together.

8 For the beak, either dab a small blob of yellow paint just below the eyes with the fine brush, or cut a short, thin strip of cereal-box card, narrow enough for a beak, and color it in with a yellow felt-tip pen.

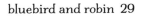

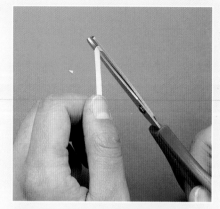

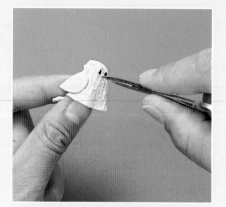

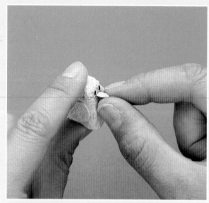

9 Snip one end of the yellow strip into a "V" and cut off the top ½ in. (1 cm) or so for the beak. Keep the rest for future birds!

10 Use the small scissors to carefully pierce a little hole for the beak under the eyes (keep the scissors closed, press down, and twist slightly from side to side). Snip the slot until it's the right size for the beak.

11 Apply a little glue inside the cone behind the slot, and push the beak into place.

tweet, tweet

Felix the Fox

Felix the Fox loves playing tricks, he's really rather sly,
he jumped out from behind a tree and made the rabbits cry.

You will need

Egg carton

Tail and paws templates (see page 124)

Craft scissors

Glue (tacky glue is best, see page 8)

Red, yellow, and white paint

Fine paintbrush

Ruler

Pencil

Fine black felt-tip or gel pen

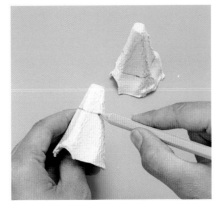

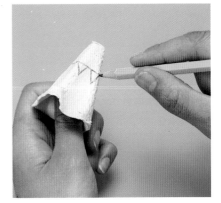

1 Roughly cut out two whole cones from an egg carton. On one, use a pencil and ruler to mark 1¾ in. (4.5 cm) from the top on each side. Join the marks with a line. This will be the body. On the other cone, mark ¾ in. (2 cm) down from the top on all sides and join with a line. This will be the head.

2 Cut out the body and put it to one side. On the head cone, choose which side you want for the face and draw two pointy ears from each corner, pointing away from the top of the cone. Make them a good size and leave a small space between the ears.

TIP

For a short cut, you could use the black pen to draw paws on the body instead of cutting them out.

3 To make the head easier to cut out, first cut along the two back corners at the base of the head to the line. Fold the flap out and cut it off.

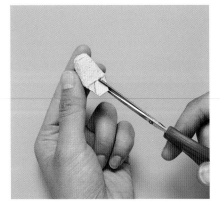

4 Roughly cut away any excess card above the ears, then snip carefully along the line and around the ears. Pull the little piece of card between the ears forward and snip it off.

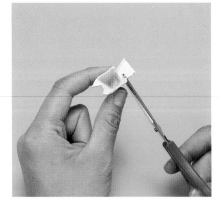

5 Cut along the back corners again, almost to the cone end, fold the flap of card back, and snip it off. Bend the ears forward very carefully.

6 Copy the tail and paws templates on page 124 onto the egg carton lid and cut out. Use the white paint to paint the face, tummy, paws, and tail tip first. When touch dry, mix orange from red and yellow, and use a fine paintbrush to add the orange markings. When the paint is dry, use a fine black pen to draw the eyes, a nose, the mouth, and claws on the paws.

7 Cut a slot up the back, long enough to fit the tail tab and push the tail into place.

8 Glue on the paws beneath the tummy. Brush glue inside the head, just on the sides, and attach to the cone body. Don't push the head right down, there should be a small gap between the top of the cone and the top of the fox's head.

bark

Oscar the Owl

**If you're searching for Oscar and can't think where to look,
he'll be in the barn, with his beak in a book.**

You will need

Egg carton

Head and tail feather templates
(see page 124)

Craft scissors

Glue (tacky glue is best, see
page 8)

Glue stick

Red, yellow, blue, and white paint

Fine paintbrush

Pencil

Plain paper

Hole punch

Fine black felt-tip or gel pen

Yellow felt-tip pen

1 The flying owl shape can be found inside an egg carton. There's a raised, molded piece for the body and egg cups either side for wings. Draw your owl shape, making sure the wing tips reach halfway down the sides of the cups. Follow the curve of the cup base for the back of the wings. Keep as much of the cardboard join with the middle cone as you can—this will be the claws.

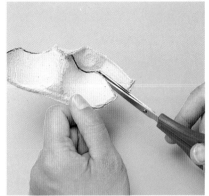

2 Cut around your shape roughly first, before carefully cutting along the line, neatening up as you go. Remember to keep the small card join for the claws.

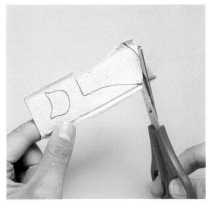

3 Copy the tail feathers and head templates on page 124 onto the egg carton lid or spare card, and cut them out.

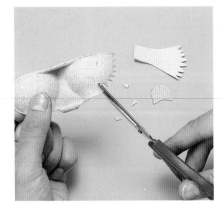

4 Snip zigzags into the end of the tail feathers, to make them look more feathery and ragged. Do the same to the wing ends on the body piece.

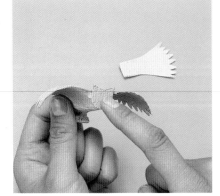

5 Glue the head onto the piece of card between the wings.

6 Glue the tail feathers on top of the body, in the groove between the wings. Trim the sides of the tail feathers if the piece doesn't fit snuggly. Push it right up to the back of the head.

7 When the glue is dry, paint your owl. Paint it brown (mix red and yellow with a little blue) and while still wet, use a fine paintbrush to dab on white spots near the end of the wings and tail feathers, for a tawny owl effect.

8 Remember to paint the underneath, too, adding chest feathers in a lighter shade. Paint the claws yellow. Allow to dry.

9 While the paint is drying, use the paper hole punch to punch two circles from some plain paper for the owl's big eyes.

TIP

If you don't have a hole punch, dot on white paint for the eyes. When dry, use the pen to add black pupils.

10 Rub a little glue stick on the head, where you want the eyes to go, then wet your finger to pick up the tiny circles and stick them down on the head. When you're happy with their position, use the fine black pen to add the pupils.

11 For the beak, color in a small piece of paper or card with a yellow felt-tip pen, cut out a little triangle, and attach in the same way as the eyes, or, instead, you could paint on a beak with a dab of yellow paint.

farmyard fun

The yard is always busy, that's just how it goes,
the animals keep Farmer Fred on his toes!

Shep the Sheepdog

**Shep is so dependable, he's happy with his lot,
and when the sneaky sheep break out, he's on it like a shot.**

You will need

Egg carton

Tail and paws templates
(see page 124)

Craft scissors

Glue (tacky glue is best,
see page 8)

Black and white paint

Fine paintbrush

Ruler

Pencil

Fine black felt-tip or gel pen

Black marker pen with a fine/
medium nib (optional)

1 Roughly cut out two whole cones from an egg carton. On one, use a pencil and ruler to mark 1¾ in. (4.5 cm) down from the top on each side. Join the marks with a line. This will be the body. On the other cone, mark ¾ in. (2 cm) down from the top on all sides and join with a line. This will be the head.

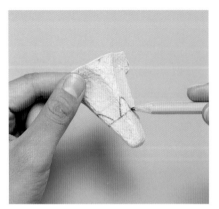

2 Cut out the body and put it to one side. On the head cone, choose which side is the face and draw two pointy ears on the corners, so half an ear is above the face and the other half is on the adjacent side. Don't draw the bottom of the ears too far down the sides or they'll be difficult to bend without ripping. Leave a space between the ears.

TIP

If your egg carton is a neutral color or white already, you could skip the white paint in step 5 and go straight to painting or drawing on the black markings.

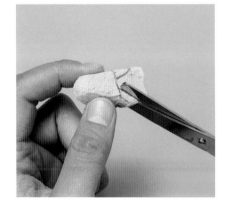

3 To make the head easier to cut out, first, cut along the two back corners at the base of the head to the line. Fold the flap back and cut it off. Roughly cut away any excess card above the ears, then cut carefully along the line and around the ears. Pull the little piece of card between the ears forward and snip it off.

4 Cut along the back corners again, almost to the cone end, fold the flap of card back, and snip it off. Bend the ears forward very carefully, taking care not to rip the card.

5 Copy the tail and paws templates on page 124 onto the egg carton lid or spare card, and cut out. Paint the face, tummy, paws, and tail tip white first. When touch dry, draw circles where you want the eyes to be and paint around them with a fine brush (or use the black marker pen).

6 On the tummy, brush on black paint (or use the pen) to make the fur look shaggy. Paint the rest of the body black and the tail too, feathering the paint around the tip.

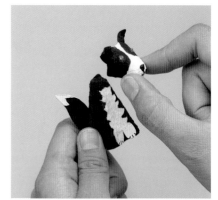

7 When the paint is dry, use a fine black pen to draw the eyes, a nose, the mouth, and claws on the paws.

8 Cut a slot up the back, long enough to fit the tail tab, and push the tail into place.

9 Glue on the paws beneath the tummy. Brush glue inside the head, just on the sides, and attach to the cone body. Don't push the head right down, there should be a small gap between the top of the cone and the top of Shep's head.

Henny the Hen

Henny dreams of dancing and starring in a show,
she twirls and spins and flaps her wings everywhere she goes.

You will need

Egg carton

Cereal-box card (optional)

Wing and tail feather templates (see page 125)

Red tissue paper

Craft scissors

Small scissors (see page 8)

Glue (tacky glue is best, see page 8)

Red, yellow, and blue paint

Fine paintbrush

Ruler

Pencil

Fine black felt-tip or gel pen

Yellow felt-tip pen (optional)

1 Roughly cut out a whole cone from the egg carton. Use a pencil and ruler to measure and mark 1¼ in. (3 cm) down from the top on each side and join the marks with a line.

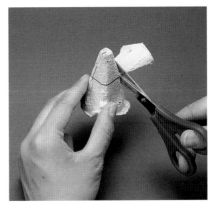

2 To help cut out the body neatly, snip up two adjacent corners to the pencil line, fold the flap back, and cut it off—it's now easier to cut along the rest of the line.

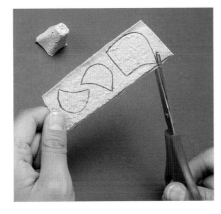

3 Copy the wing and tail feather templates from page 125 onto the egg carton lid and cut out carefully.

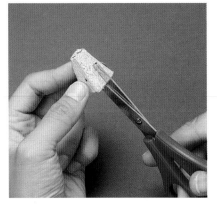

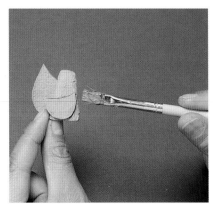

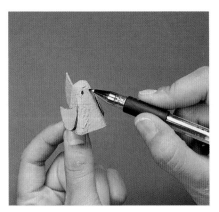

4 Cut a slot up the middle of one of the cone sides, almost to the top, then snip out an extra sliver to widen the slot slightly, and check the tail feather fits. Trim the bottom of the tail feather piece if you need to.

5 Dab a little glue on each wing and stick them either side of the body. When the glue is dry, paint your hen brown (mix yellow, red, and a small dab of blue). While the paint is drying, why not make a nest and some eggs (see page 44)?

6 When the paint is dry, use a fine black pen to dot eyes near the very top of the cone. Keep them small and quite close together.

7 For the beak, either dab a small blob of yellow paint just below the eyes with a fine brush, then go to step 9, or cut a short, thin strip of cereal-box card, narrow enough for a beak, and color it in with a yellow felt-tip pen. Snip one end into a "V" and cut off the top ½ in. (1 cm) or so for the beak. Keep the rest for future hens!

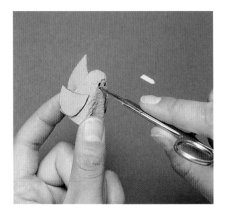

8 Use the small scissors to carefully pierce a little hole for the beak under the eyes (keep the scissors closed, press down, and twist slightly from side to side). Snip the slot until it's the right size for the beak. Apply a little glue inside the cone, behind the slot, and push the beak into place.

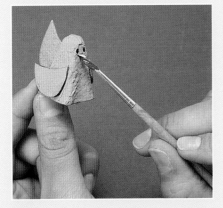

9 Add a dot of red paint under the beak for the hen's wattle.

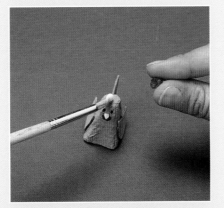

10 Cut out a small square of red tissue paper, about ¾ x ¾ in. (2 x 2 cm), and scrunch it up to make the hen's head comb. Glue on top of the head.

TIP

Why not have a go at making different types of hens or come up with your own colorful breed!

cluck, cluck, cluck

Nest of Eggs

Make a clutch of eggs for the hens to brood over!

You will need

Egg carton

3 sheets of tissue paper
(2 yellow, 1 orange)

Modeling clay (plasticine)

Glue

Long scissors

Craft scissors

1 Loosely fold the sheets of tissue paper together, so you can easily cut across the width with one snip of your long scissors. Keep the strips as thin as you can.

2 Unfurl the strips and tear or cut them up until you have a good quantity of different lengths of yellow and orange strands.

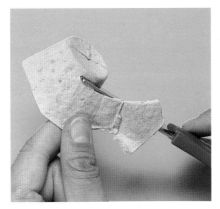

3 For the nest, cut an egg cup from the egg carton and trim it down to make a shallow dish shape.

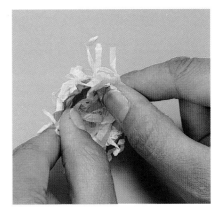

4 Brush a layer of glue inside the nest and around the rim. Then use your thumbs to press a good pinch of tissue paper strands into the glue.

5 Now brush glue on the outside of the nest, and press on more tissue-paper strands. Pat them into the glue and press around the shape of the nest, until it is well covered. Trim any stray strands, but leave a few for a natural look.

6 Roll a small piece of modeling clay into an oval shape to make an egg. Old, mixed-up modeling clay makes great speckled eggs! Put them in the nest or add a few to the hen house (see page 80) to keep the hens happy.

TIP

Use any leftover strands to make hay bales and hay stacks (see page 110), or for bedding in the stables or pigsty.

Ron the Rooster

The animals are fed up with Ron's cock-a-doodle-doos, they've had enough of early starts and want a morning snooze!

You will need

Egg carton

Cereal-box card (optional)

Red tissue paper

Wing and tail feather templates (see page 125)

Craft scissors

Small scissors (see page 8) (optional)

Glue

Green, red, and yellow paint

Fine paintbrush

Ruler

Pencil

Fine black felt-tip or gel pen

Orange felt-tip pen (optional)

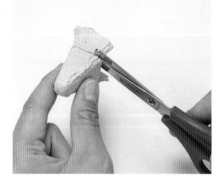

1 Roughly cut out a whole cone from the egg carton. Use a pencil and ruler to measure and mark 1½ in. (3.5 cm) down from the top on each side and join the marks with a line. To help cut out the body neatly, snip up two adjacent corners to the pencil line, fold the flap back, and cut it off—it's now easier to cut along the rest of the line.

2 Copy the templates on page 125 onto the egg carton lid, and cut out. For the tail feathers, cut out the basic shape first, then draw on the feathery detail following the dotted lines on the template. Snip out the little triangles.

3 Cut a slot up the middle of one of the cone sides, almost to the top, then snip out an extra sliver to widen the slot slightly, and check the tail feather fits. Trim the bottom of the tail feather piece if you need to.

4 Paint your rooster body and tail feathers. Ron has green, orange, and yellow stripes with a dash of red. Paint the wings separately, too.

5 When the paint is dry, use a fine black pen to dot eyes near the very top of the cone. Keep them small and quite close together.

6 For the beak, either dab a small blob of orange paint just below the eyes with a fine brush then go to step 8, or cut a short, thin strip of cereal-box card, narrow enough for a beak, and color it in with an orange felt-tip pen. Snip one end into a "V" and cut off the top ½ in. (1 cm) or so for the beak. Keep the rest for future birds!

7 Use the small scissors to carefully pierce a little hole for the beak under the eyes (keep the scissors closed, press down, and twist slightly from side to side). Snip the slot until it's the right size for the beak. Apply a little glue inside the cone, behind the slot, and push the beak into place.

8 Add a dot of red paint under the beak for the wattle.

9 Cut out a small square of red tissue paper, about ¾ x ¾ in. (2 x 2 cm), and scrunch it up to make a head comb. Glue the comb on top of the head and glue the wings either side of the body.

cock-a-doodle-doo!

Dilly the Duck

**Silly billy Dilly Duck, never has the greatest luck.
When she took a trip away, she caught the flu on her first day!**

You will need

Egg carton

Head template (see page 126)

White and yellow paint

Fine paintbrush

Glue

Craft scissors

Pencil

Ruler

Fine black felt-tip or gel pen

1 Roughly cut out a whole cone from the egg carton. Use a pencil and ruler to measure and mark 1½ in. (3.5 cm) down from the top on each side and join the marks with a line. To help cut out the body neatly, snip up two adjacent corners to the pencil line, fold the flap back, and cut it off—it's now easier to cut along the rest of the line.

2 Cut the cone in half, lengthwise. This will give you two duck bodies.

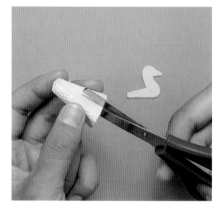

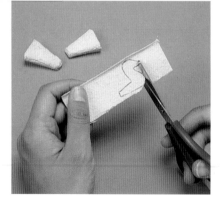

3 Copy the template on page 126 onto the egg carton lid or a spare piece of card, and cut out the head carefully—this is tricky cutting but worth it!

4 Cut a slot on the wide end of the body for the head. Snip out an extra sliver to widen the slot. The neck should slide in, almost to the front, with some of the duck's chest visible below. If the body doesn't sit completely flat, trim the bottom of the head piece.

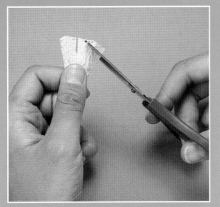

5 Take the head out and flatten the wide end of the body with your finger and thumb, so you can cut the corners off at a slant on both sides. Cut to the central slot and don't take too much off.

6 Brush some glue behind the body slot and push the head back into place.

7 When the glue is dry, paint your duck white and the beak yellow. Use a fine black pen to dot on eyes either side of the head when the paint is dry.

Pampered Pigs

The pigs are into pampering and usually begin with a cleansing mud bath "that does wonders for the skin!"

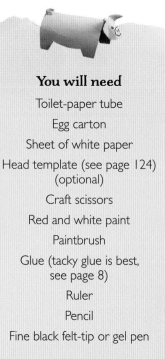

You will need

Toilet-paper tube

Egg carton

Sheet of white paper

Head template (see page 124) (optional)

Craft scissors

Red and white paint

Paintbrush

Glue (tacky glue is best, see page 8)

Ruler

Pencil

Fine black felt-tip or gel pen

1 First, paint the toilet-paper tube pink all over (mix the perfect shade from red and white).

2 While the paint is drying, make a head for your pig from the little rounded cardboard catch on an egg carton—it's a great shape for a snout. Cut off the flap with the catch from the carton.

oink

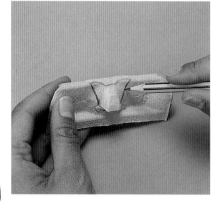

3 Use a pencil to draw sloping lines either side of the catch, right up to the top of the piece of card. Slope the lines back down and inward to form the ears, and join them in the middle. If you don't have a carton with a catch like this, then use the template on page 124.

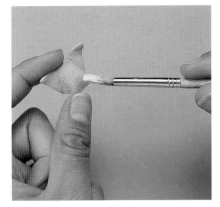

4 Carefully cut out the head and paint it pink all over, to match the body.

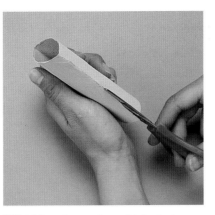

5 When the cardboard tube is dry, squeeze the sides together to make crease lines. Cut along the creases so you have two pieces of pink card.

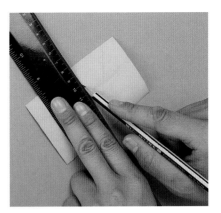

6 Take one of the pieces (keep the other for your next pig) and with a long side facing you, use a ruler and pencil to draw a line roughly down the center of the card to divide it in two. Don't cut it.

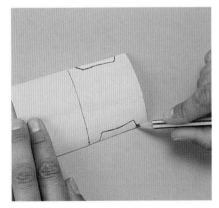

7 For the legs, work on one side of the line only. About ¼ in. (1 cm) in from a corner, draw a short sloping line and do the same ¼ in. (1 cm) in from the pencil line. Join the lines with a gentle curve for the pig's belly. Repeat on the opposite side of the card, making sure both look similar before cutting out the small piece between the legs.

8 To position the head, squeeze the card body back into its curved tube shape, set it on a flat surface, and at the top of the curve on the legless end, make two pencil marks, roughly ¼ in. (1 cm) apart.

TIP

While you're waiting for the paint to dry, why not make a trough (see page 112) for your pigs to feed from?

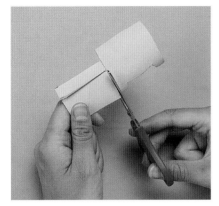

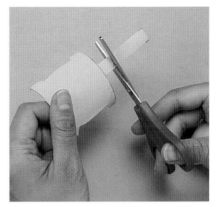

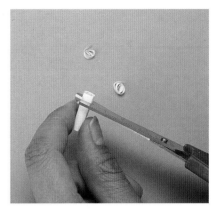

9 From these marks, cut straight down to the pencil line. Then cut away the two side pieces by cutting along the pencil line, so you're left with a long strip in the middle.

10 Snip most of the strip off, leaving a small tab about ½ in. (1.5 cm) long for attaching to the head.

11 For the curly tail, cut a small rectangle of white paper, about 1 x 2 in. (3 x 5 cm), and roll it tightly lengthwise. Snip a thin strip off the end of the roll—use your fingers and thumb to push the paper swirl back into a more rounded shape and let it unfurl a little.

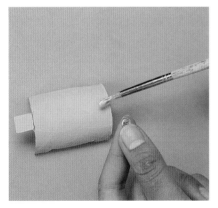

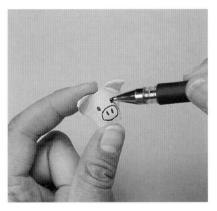

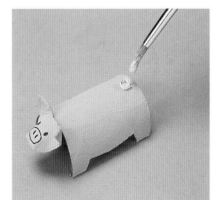

12 Brush a small dab of glue on the back end of your pig's body, and stick the tail in place.

13 The head should be dry now— use a fine black pen to draw the eyes and a snout. Bend the ears forward a little. Glue the head to the tab.

14 When the glue holding the tail is set, carefully dab on a little pink paint to finish the curly tail.

Corky the Cat

Corky cat could sleep all day if given half a chance,
even mice that come too close won't get a second glance.

You will need

A cork

Cereal-box card, 5 x 5 in.
(12 x12 cm)

Head template (see page 124)

Strong all-purpose glue

Clothes pin (peg)

Black and white paint (or your
chosen colors)

Fine paintbrush

Craft scissors

Ruler

Pencil

Black marker pen with a fine/
medium nib (optional)

Fine black felt-tip or gel pen

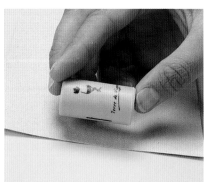

1 Draw a line along the length of the
cork with the black pen, and place the
cork on the card, with the line touching
the card edge.

2 Slowly roll the cork forward a little,
and use a pencil to mark the card at
both ends of the cork. Keep rolling and
marking, until the black line on the cork is
touching the card again, on the other side.
Make a mark here, too.

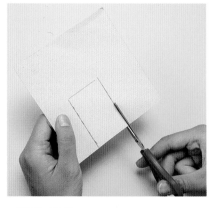

3 Join the marks using a ruler to make
a rectangle and cut out the strip of
card. This is going to be the cat's body.

meow

4 At each end of the strip of card, draw a pair of short legs with a curved line for the tummy in between, as shown. Try to make both ends as similar as possible.

5 Carefully cut around the legs and tummy following the lines.

6 Position the cork on its end in a corner of the spare card, and draw around it to make a circle. Add a short tab from the circle to the edge of the card (the head will be attached here).

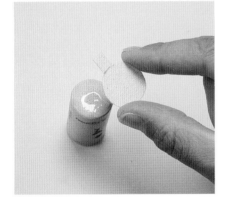

7 Cut out the circle and tab in one piece and glue it to the cork end using strong glue.

8 Cut a thin strip of card for a tail, making it a little longer than you want the tail to be, and taper it at one end. Copy the head template on page 124 and carefully cut this out, too.

9 Spread an even layer of strong glue on the back of the card body (but not the legs) and place the tail halfway along one edge, with the plain side facing down.

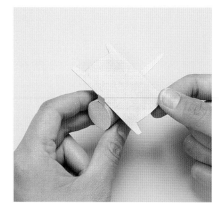

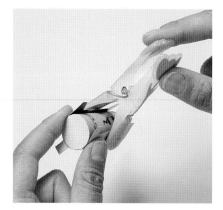

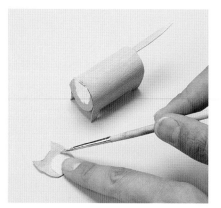

10 Line the tail up with the head tab and stick the body tightly around the cork.

11 Use a clothes pin (peg) between the legs to hold the card in place. If the cork is too wide for your pin (peg), lay the cat on its side and lean a book on the body, to hold the card down while the glue dries.

12 When the glue is dry, remove the clothes pin, bend the legs back into place, and trim if necessary so it stands steady. Mix your paint colors and paint your cat. If you want a stripy cat, use a lighter color first. Paint around the top of the head, too.

13 For a tabby cat, add darker stripes over the top of the body with a fine paintbrush or a marker pen. Don't forget the tail!

14 Use the fine black pen to draw the cat's eyes, nose, mouth, and whiskers. Bend the head tab down firmly and glue on the head.

TIP

For a marmalade cat, mix orange from red and yellow, and paint darker stripes to give your cat its unique markings.

Cooing Doves

**The doves are such a gentle bunch, they're really calm and kind,
they like to coo their cares away and do yoga to unwind.**

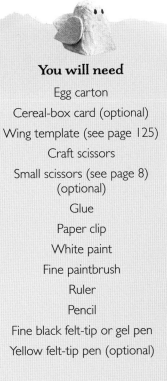

You will need

Egg carton

Cereal-box card (optional)

Wing template (see page 125)

Craft scissors

Small scissors (see page 8)
(optional)

Glue

Paper clip

White paint

Fine paintbrush

Ruler

Pencil

Fine black felt-tip or gel pen

Yellow felt-tip pen (optional)

1 To make the body, roughly cut out a whole cone from the egg carton, so it's easier to work with. Use a pencil to mark ¾ in. (2 cm) down from the top on all sides and join the marks with a line.

2 Snip up all four corners to the line. Bend back the four flaps. Cut three of them off, leaving one flap still attached for the tail feathers.

3 Trim the remaining flap to about ½ in. (1 cm) long and round off the corners a little, for a more curved fantail.

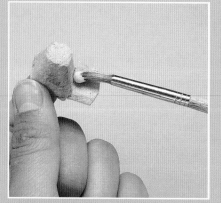

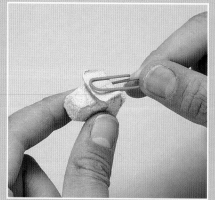

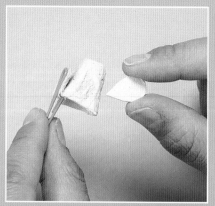

4 Apply glue along the tail feather crease (where it joins the body). Try not to get any glue on the top part of the fantail.

5 Fold up the fantail to glue the bottom part to the body, and attach a paper clip to hold it in place while the glue dries.

6 Copy the template on page 125 and cut out two wings from the egg carton lid or a piece of spare card. Brush a little glue on the wings and stick them either side of the body.

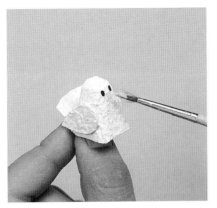

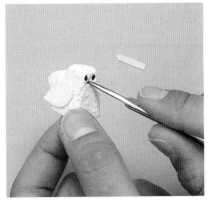

7 When the glue is dry, remove the paper clip and paint your dove white. Popping the cone on a finger is a good way to make sure you've painted all the edges—although you may end up with a painted finger too!

8 When the paint is dry, use a fine black pen to dot eyes near the very top of the cone. Keep them small and quite close together. For the beak, either dab a small blob of yellow paint just below the eyes with the fine brush then go to step 11, or cut a short, thin strip of cereal-box card, narrow enough for a beak, and color it in with a yellow felt-tip pen.

9 Snip one end of the yellow strip into a "V" and cut off the top ½ in. (1 cm) or so for the beak. Keep the rest for future birds! Use the small scissors to carefully pierce a little hole for the beak under the eyes (keep the scissors closed, press down, and twist slightly from side to side). Snip the slot until it's the right size for the beak.

10 Apply a little glue inside the cone behind the slot, and push the beak into place.

11 When the glue is dry, bend the top part of the fantail back a little. Your dove is ready to relax in the dovecote (see page 90).

TIP

Make some more doves so they can coo at each other across the farmyard. Paint some of them pale gray, too.

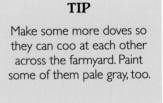

home sweet home

At the end of the day, it's got to be said, there's nothing quite like a warm, cozy bed.

Farmer Fred

Farmer Fred gets out of bed early in the morning, and by the time his jobs are done, he really can't stop yawning.

You will need

Egg carton

Craft scissors

Glue

Paint

Fine paintbrush

Ruler

Pencil

Fine black felt-tip or gel pen

Red felt-tip or gel pen

1 Roughly cut out three whole cones from the egg carton. Use a pencil and ruler to mark 1¾ in. (4.5 cm) from the top on each side of one cone. Join the marks with a line. On the second cone, mark the line 1¼ in. (3 cm) down from the top, and make it 1 in. (2.5 cm) on the third one. Cut out all three cone pieces. To help cut them out neatly, snip up two adjacent corners to the pencil line, fold the flap back, and cut it off— it's now easier to cut along the rest of the line.

2 To make the legs, take the largest cone. Cut up the middle of one side, about two thirds of the way to the top, then snip straight across to each corner. Do the same on the opposite side.

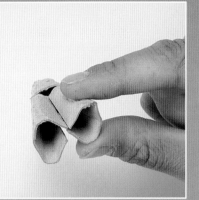

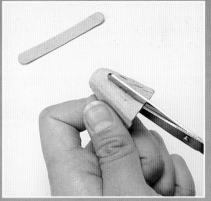

3 Press the cut card edges inward, toward each other to define the legs, and gently squeeze and round each one. You should end up with a good pair of flares!

4 Cut a narrow strip of card, about ¼ in. (5 mm) wide and 2½ in. (6 cm) long, from the egg carton lid for the arms, and round off each end for the hands. Take the 1¼ in. (3 cm) cone (this will be the body) and cut slots up two opposite sides, almost to the top.

5 Slot the arm piece into the body, and when it looks equal on both sides, press the middle of the card strip back, inside the cone, to bring the arms forward.

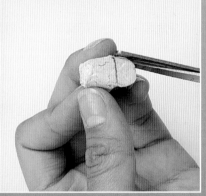

6 For the head, draw a rough pencil line around the remaining cone, about halfway up. Don't worry if the line is a bit wobbly, it's only a guide. Cut up all four corners to the line. Bend back three of the flaps and cut them off.

7 Trim and round off the edges of the remaining flap to make a beard shape.

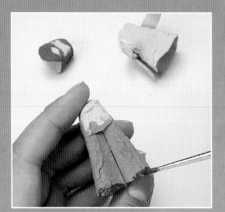
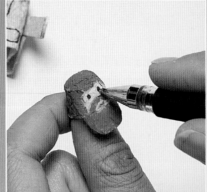

8 Paint each piece of your farmer separately, using any colors you like—make a shirt or jacket for the body, and pants (trousers) or jeans for the legs. Mix a pale skin color with a little red, yellow, and white, or for a darker skin tone, add a little blue. Paint the hair and beard too.

9 When the paint is dry, use the red pen to add a mouth and a fine black pen to add eyes and any details you want to the farmer's clothes, such as buttons or pockets on his jacket.

10 Glue the head onto the body, then glue the body to the legs, or leave the legs unglued so you can arrange the farmer in a sitting position in the tractor on page 99.

hello

hello

Winnie the Farmer's Wife

The farm runs like clockwork and that's thanks to Winnie, who keeps lists of chores in the front pocket of her pinny.

You will need

Egg carton

Craft scissors

Glue

Paint

Fine paintbrush

Ruler

Pencil

Fine black felt-tip or gel pen

Red felt-tip or gel pen

1 Roughly cut out three whole cones from the egg carton. Use a pencil and ruler to mark 1½ in. (4 cm) from the top on each side of one cone. Join the marks with a line. On the second cone, mark the line 1 in. (2.5 cm) down from the top, and make it ¾ in. (2 cm) on the third one. Cut out all three cone pieces. To help cut them out neatly, snip up two adjacent corners to the pencil line, fold the flap back, and cut it off—it's now easier to cut along the rest of the line.

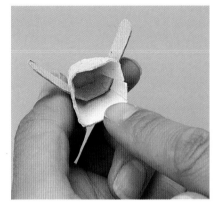

2 Cut a narrow strip of card, about ¼ in. (5 mm) wide and 2½ in. (6 cm) long, from the egg carton lid for the arms, and round off each end for the hands. Take the ¾ in. (2 cm) cone (this will be the body) and cut slots up two opposite sides, almost to the top. Slot the arm piece into the body, and when it looks equal on both sides, press the middle of the card strip back, inside the cone, to bring the arms forward.

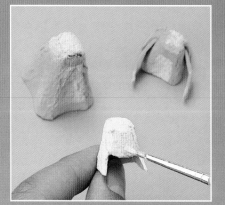

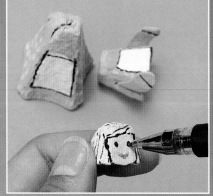

3 For the head, take the 1 in. (2.5 cm) cone, and draw a rough pencil line around it, about halfway up. Don't worry if the line is a bit wobbly, it's only a guide. Cut up all four corners to the line. Bend back one of the flaps and cut it off—this will be the face.

4 Paint each piece of Winnie separately, using any colors you like. The biggest cone is Winnie's skirt—we've given her a pinny. Mix a pale skin color with a little red, yellow, and white, or for a darker skin tone, add a little blue. Paint the hair too—you could give Winnie fashionable bangs (a fringe), or a side parting!

5 When the paint is dry, give Winnie a haircut if you want, or leave her hair long. Use the fine black pen to add eyes and any details you like to her hair and clothes. Draw a smile with the red pen.

6 Glue the head onto the body, then glue the body to the skirt.

Farmhouse

This little house makes a sweet addition to the farm, with its porch and rambling rose by the front door. The colors and details are a guide only, so have fun designing your own farmhouse, if you'd like.

You will need

2 cereal boxes (maximum width 10 in./25 cm)

Blue and white paper

Adhesive postage labels

Paper clips

Long scissors

Craft scissors

Glue

Glue stick

Paint

Big paintbrush

Ruler

Pencil

Fine black felt-tip or gel pen

Black marker pen with fine/ medium nib

Brad (paper fastener) (optional)

Colored tissue paper (optional)

Small scissors (see page 8) (optional)

1 Take one cereal box and use the marker pen and ruler to mark each corner, 7 in. (18 cm) up from the base. Cut down the corners from the top to each mark.

2 Bend back the front and back pieces of card and press firmly along the creases. Cut most of the card away, leaving flaps about ¾ in. (2 cm) wide. The roof will be glued to these later.

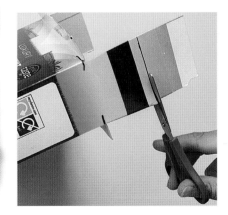

3 On both sides of the box, measure and mark 9 in. (23 cm) up from the base and cut straight across the card here.

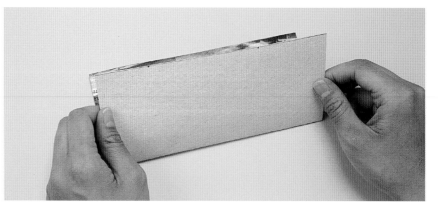

4 Mark the halfway point along the top edge of both short sides, and cut down from this mark to each corner to make a triangle shape.

5 Cut a rectangle for the roof from the other cereal packet. It should be a little longer than the width of your farmhouse front, by about ¾ in. (2 cm). For the depth, measure one side of the triangle you've just made, double it, and add 2 in. (5 cm). Fold the card rectangle in half, lengthwise.

6 Mix a dark gray and paint the whole roof. Put it to one side to dry.

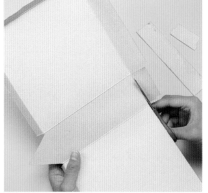

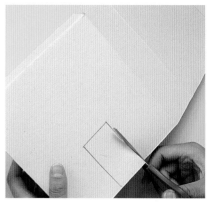

7 Open up the base of the box and carefully open the side seam, too. (Don't use scissors, instead slide your fingers or a ruler up the seam to keep as much of it intact as possible.) Cut away all the flaps at the base of the box.

8 With the plain inside of the box facing you, choose the side you want for the front of your farmhouse and, with a pencil, make a mark halfway along the edge. Then, draw vertical lines ¾ in. (2 cm) either side of the mark, that are 2¾ in. (7 cm) long, and join them at the top with a straight line. Cut up one side only and along the top (so that your door opens).

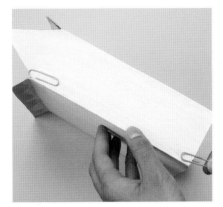

9 Mix up a color for your house and paint it all over, or leave it the natural cardboard color. Choose a color for the front door and paint it, too. For the chimneys, cut a strip about 3 in. (8 cm) long and 1 in. (3 cm) wide from some spare card. Paint this strip the same color as your house.

10 Turn the farmhouse box inside out, bending the folds the opposite way, and glue the seam again. Attach paper clips to the top and bottom to hold the seam in place. Put the box on its side, with a heavy book or something similar inside, pressing down on the seam while the glue dries.

11 If you'd like a tiled or shingled roof, use the fine black pen and a ruler to draw evenly spaced lines across the roof. Then add downward strokes for a tiled effect.

TIP

Try using a pastry brush to paint the larger pieces— it's really flexible and easy to use!

12 For the chimney slots, makes cuts in the roof fold at both ends. Make them a little longer than the width of the chimney strip. Cut the chimney strip in half.

13 On the farmhouse, bend the front and back roof flaps outward, pressing along the folds as firmly as you can. Brush glue on the flaps, then line up the top of the roof with the tip of the triangles, and attach the roof. Use paper clips to hold it in place while the glue dries.

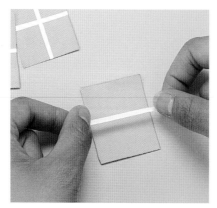

14 For windows, cut a strip from one end of the sheet of blue paper, about 6 × 2 in. (16 × 5 cm). Fold the strip in half and cut along the crease. Fold each piece in half again and cut along the creases. This will give you four matching windows.

15 For the window bars, cut thin strips from a sticky postage label, remove the backing paper, and make a cross on each window. Fold any overlapping ends to the back of the paper. (If you don't have postage labels, cut thin strips of plain paper and use a glue stick.)

16 If you'd like a frame for your windows, cut an 8 × 2½ in. (20 × 6 cm) strip of plain white paper. Fold the strip in half and cut along the crease. Fold each piece in half again and cut along the creases. Use a glue stick to glue the windows in the middle of the frames.

TIP

If you have a bigger cereal box that's over 10 in. (25 cm) wide, you will need to scale up the size of the door and windows, too.

17 Place your windows where you'd like them and lightly mark their position with a pencil. Rub a glue stick on the back of the windows and glue in place. Use a brad (paper fastener) for a door knob if you have one, making a hole with the closed ends of a pair of small scissors and twisting from side to side. Paint on a door knob if you don't have a brad.

18 For a porch, paint or color in a thin strip of plain paper about 2½ in. (6 cm) long. Fold and cut it in half. Rub glue stick on the back of each piece and stick them above the door in an upside down "V" shape.

19 To add a cottage rose by the front door, scrunch up small bits of colored tissue paper. Brush glue where you want the rose to ramble, and arrange the tissue paper pieces.

20 Finish your house by brushing some glue under the chimney slots in the roof, and then push the two chimney pieces into place.

Stable

For the stable, it's best to use a cereal box that has wide sides, so the horses can fit inside and enjoy their new home in comfort.

You will need

Cereal box with wide sides

Long scissors

Craft scissors

Paper clips

Sticky tape

Glue

Black, white, red, yellow, and blue paint

Big paintbrush

Ruler

Pencil

Black marker pen with a fine/medium nib

Fine black felt-tip or gel pen

1 Use the marker pen and ruler to mark 5 in. (13 cm) up from the base on the two front corners of the cereal box. Then mark 6 in. (15 cm) up from the base on the two back corners. Use a ruler to join the marks on the box sides, with a sloped line.

2 Cut down the four corners from the top of the box to each mark. Bend back the front and back pieces of card and press firmly along the creases. Cut most of the card away, leaving flaps about ½ in. (1 cm) wide on the front and back. The roof will be glued to these later.

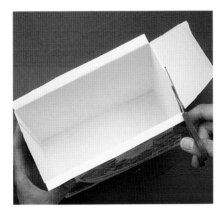

3 On both sides of the box, cut along the sloped line.

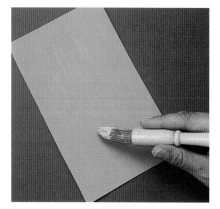

4 Cut a rectangle for the roof from some spare cereal-box card. It should be a little longer than the width of your stable front, by about ¾ in. (2 cm). For the depth, measure the length of the slope and add 1½ in. (3 cm). Mix a gray and paint the plain side of the rectangle. Put it to one side to dry.

5 Open up the base of the box and carefully open the side seam, too. (Don't use scissors, instead slide your fingers or a ruler up the seam to keep as much of it intact as possible.) Cut away all the flaps at the base of the box.

6 Mix red and yellow paint with a dab of blue to make brown. Use a big brush to paint the stable. Even, downward strokes give a good, grainy wood effect.

7 If you'd like to add the effect of wooden slats, or tongue and groove, to your stable, when the paint is dry, use a ruler to draw evenly spaced vertical lines with the fine black pen along the whole of the flattened box.

8 To add the stable doors to the front, draw two evenly spaced rectangles, about 4½ × 2½ in. (11 × 6 cm). You could add more doors if your box is very wide. Cut up one side of the door and along the top (so that it opens). Draw a line across the door, about 2½ in. (6 cm) up from the base and cut along the line, so the top part opens separately.

9 Use the black marker pen to draw bolts on the stable doors—make sure the end of the line extends across the door opening.

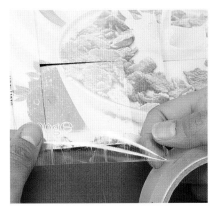

10 Put some sticky tape across the back of one of the doors to hold the lower part closed. This will make the stable sturdier.

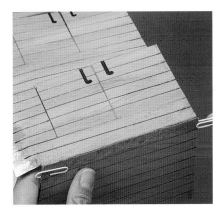

11 Turn the cereal-box stable inside out (so that the painted side is facing out), bending the folds the opposite way, and glue the seam again. Attach paper clips to the top and bottom to hold the seam in place. Put the box on its side, with a heavy book or something similar inside, pressing down on the seam while the glue dries.

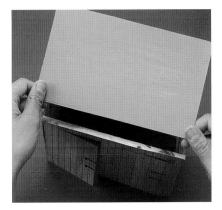

12 When the glue is dry, bend the front and back roof flaps outward, pressing along the folds as firmly as you can. Brush glue on the flaps and attach the roof. Use paper clips to hold it in position while the glue dries.

13 Add some bedding and some hay (see page 110) and your stable is ready!

stable 75

Barn

This open-sided barn is a perfect animal shelter or stack it up with hay bales at harvest time!

You will need

Cereal box (maximum width
9 in./23 cm)

Cereal-box card, 5 × 6 in.
(12 × 15 cm)

Sandpaper

Paper clips

Paint

Big paintbrush

Glue

Long scissors

Craft scissors

Ruler

Black marker pen with a fine/
medium nib

Fine black felt-tip or gel pen

1 Use a black marker pen and a ruler to mark 10 in. (25 cm) up from the base on all four corners of the cereal box. Cut down the corners from the top to these marks.

2 Fold back the card pieces on all four sides and press firmly along the creases. Cut some of the card away, leaving flaps about 2 in. (5 cm) wide.

3 Carefully open up the base of the box, keeping all the flaps intact, and collapse the box so it is flat.

4 Use the black marker pen and ruler to draw a line along the length of both sides (including the flaps), about a third of the way up from the edge. Cut along the lines to separate the box into two pieces. The part with the shorter sides is going to be the floor of the barn.

5 Cut the end flaps of the barn floor so they are the same height as the sides. Turn the card over to the shiny, printed side, and use a small piece of sandpaper to rub away some of the sheen along the four sides—this will make them easier to paint later. There is no need to sand the middle of the box.

6 Turn the box over to the plain, cardboard side again, brush glue on the flaps, and reconstruct the box shape. Use paper clips to hold the corners in place while the glue dries.

7 While the glue is drying, work on the other half of the cereal box to make the roof. Cut the end flaps so that they are the same height as the sides (don't worry if they're a little shorter). Paint the plain, cardboard side in your chosen roof color—we used a traditional red. Put to one side to dry.

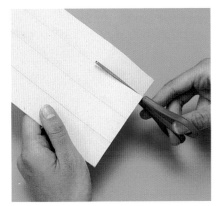

8 For the posts to hold up the roof, take the rectangle of cereal-box card. Mark 1¼ in. (3 cm) intervals along the shorter sides and join the marks so you end up with four equal strips. Rub sandpaper over the shiny, printed side of the card to make it easier to paint later, then cut out the strips.

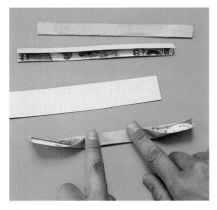

9 Fold the strips in half lengthwise, with the plain card side on the outside, to make the corner posts. Press firmly along the crease line.

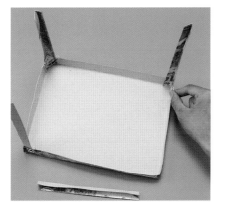

10 When the glue is dry on the barn base, remove the paper clips. Brush glue in the corners, press the posts into place and use paper clips on either side of each post to hold them in position while the glue dries.

11 On the roof section, if you'd like a corrugated effect, use the fine black pen and ruler to draw evenly spaced lines across it. Don't forget the end flaps.

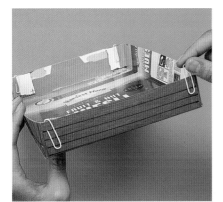

12 Reconstruct the box shape, but inside out this time. Brush glue on the flaps and use paper clips to hold them in place.

13 When the posts are firmly attached to the base, remove the paper clips and paint the bottom edges and posts in gray. Paint the inside too, if you want.

14 When the paint is dry, cut an opening in the base edge, following the crease, and set the roof on top of the posts. It's ready for some hay bales and the tractor (see pages 99 and 110)!

Hen House

The hen house is made using a fun paper-folding technique that can be scaled up to make other small outbuildings.

You will need

Egg carton

Sheet of colored paper

Paint

Big paintbrush

Craft scissors

Ruler

Pencil

Fine black felt-tip or gel pen

Glue stick

Paper clips

1 Cut the lid off the egg carton and paint it the same color as the paper you've chosen for the hen house. We painted our hen house brown, mixed from red, yellow, and a dab of blue paint.

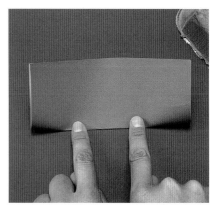

2 While the paint is drying, cut a 5 x 6 in. (13 x 15 cm) rectangle from the sheet of colored paper and fold it in half lengthwise.

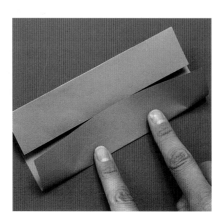

3 Open the paper out flat and fold the top and bottom edges inward, so they meet in the middle on the crease line. Press down firmly along the folds.

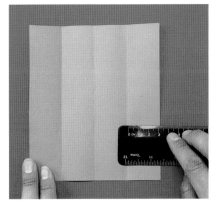

4 Open the paper out flat again, and measure the distance from the edge of the paper to the nearest fold. Make a note of this measurement.

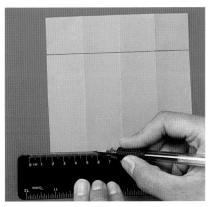

5 Turn the piece of paper over with the crease lines running vertically. Use the black pen and ruler to draw a line across the top and another across the bottom that are the same distance from the edge as the measurement noted earlier. Press down firmly with the pen to help make folding easier.

6 Turn the piece of paper over again and fold firmly along the marked black lines. Open out the paper and snip up the three short crease lines, up to the marked line, to make tabs. Do this on both sides.

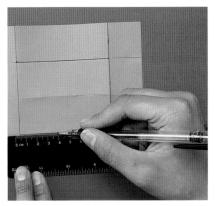

7 Now it's time to decorate the hen house. First, join the black marked lines by drawing along the crease lines in between them to make a rectangle. This will be the roof.

8 If you'd like to add the effect of wooden slats, or tongue and groove, use the pen and ruler to draw evenly spaced lines across the whole piece of paper. Alternatively, you could color in the roof.

9 Draw two arched openings on one side edge. Carefully cut them out. We've also drawn little hearts above the arches.

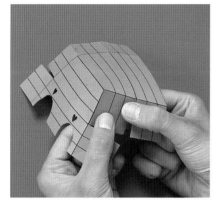

10 Rub an even layer of glue stick all over one middle tab, then bring the other middle tab across it, until the top edges line up and the roof takes shape. Press them together. Do the same at the other end.

11 Apply glue to the pointy lower half of the roof tab, and down the edge of one wall tab. Then bring the wall tabs together, so they cross over and the bottom edges line up. (Don't worry if the top edges don't line up perfectly, it's more important that the base is even.) Repeat at the other end. Use paper clips to hold the walls in place, if you need to.

12 When the egg box lid is dry, use a pencil to draw an arch from one corner, up to the top of the lid, and back down to the next corner. Then leave a gap of about ½ in. (1 cm) at the bottom (for the leg supports), before drawing another arch on the adjacent side. Repeat on all sides. Try to draw around any molded parts of the lid you don't want, and keep the arches as even as possible. Cut along the pencil lines.

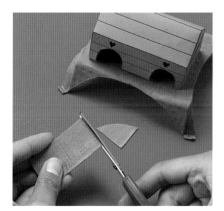

14 Pop a nest and some straw inside so your hens can feel at home and start laying eggs (see page 44).

13 Use a piece of painted card cut from the lid to make a ramp for your hens, and draw lines across it for the struts.

Kennel

The kennel is made using the same technique as the hen house. Once you've got the hang of it, you may want to make more than one!

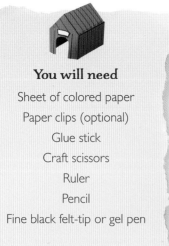

You will need

Sheet of colored paper

Paper clips (optional)

Glue stick

Craft scissors

Ruler

Pencil

Fine black felt-tip or gel pen

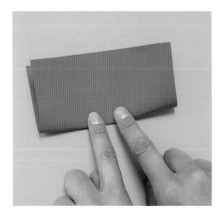

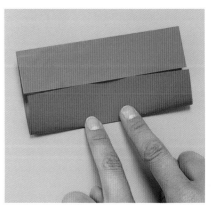

1 Cut a 5 x 5 in. (13 x 13 cm) square from the sheet of colored paper and fold it in half, making a firm crease with your fingers.

2 Open the paper out flat and fold the top and bottom edges inward, so they meet in the middle on the crease line. Press down firmly along the folds.

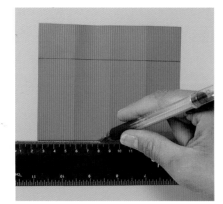

3 Open the paper out flat again, and measure the distance from the edge of the paper to the nearest fold. Make a note of this measurement.

4 Turn the piece of paper over with the crease lines running vertically. Use the black pen and ruler to draw a line across the top and another across the bottom that are the same distance from the edge as the measurement noted earlier. Press down firmly with the pen to help make folding easier.

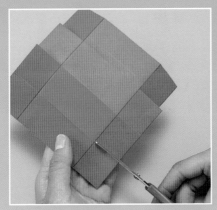

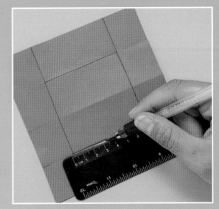

5 Turn the piece of paper over again and fold firmly along the marked black lines.

6 Open out the paper and snip up the three short crease lines, up to the marked line, to make tabs. Do this on both sides.

7 Now it's time to decorate the kennel. First, join the black marked lines by drawing along the crease lines in between them to make a square. This will be the roof.

woof

SHEP

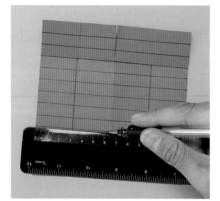

8 If you'd like to add the effect of wooden slats, or tongue and groove, use the pen and ruler to draw evenly spaced lines across the whole piece of paper. Alternatively, you could color-in the roof.

9 Rub an even layer of glue stick all over one middle tab, then bring the other middle tab across it, until the top edges line up and the roof takes shape. Press them together. Do the same at the other end.

10 Apply glue to the pointy lower half of the roof tab, and down the edge of one wall tab. Then bring the wall tabs together, so they cross over and the bottom edges line up. (Don't worry if the top edges don't line up perfectly, it's more important that the base is even.) Repeat at the other end. Use paper clips to hold the walls in place, if you need to.

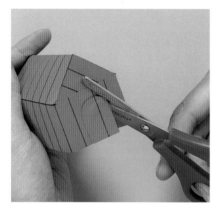

11 When the glue is dry, draw and cut out an arched opening for your dog at one end of the kennel. You could also make a little name plaque to put above it. We also added black dots as "nails" on the roof.

TIP

Make a bowl and bone from modeling clay (plasticine), to keep Shep happy when he's at home.

Pigsty

The pigs love to have their own space to wallow and play, and when it is time for a nap they can rest under the roofed shelter.

You will need

Cereal box

Sheet of colored paper

Sandpaper

Paper clips

Black, white, red, yellow, and blue paint

Big paintbrush

Glue

Glue stick

Long scissors

Craft scissors

Ruler

Black marker pen with a fine/medium nib

Fine black felt-tip or gel pen

1 Make sure your cereal box still has two side flaps at the top (you'll need them later). Cut away the long flaps on the front and back.

2 To make the sides easier to paint later, rub them with some sandpaper to roughen the shiny surface. You don't need to sand the front and back of the box.

3 Use the black marker pen and ruler to draw a line across the front of the box, 3 in. (8 cm) up from the base. Cut down the corners from the top to the line, bend the card back, and cut along the line to remove the front section.

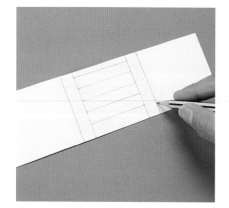

4 Take the piece of card you've just cut out and make an end wall for your pigsty—it will already be the right width. Measure and cut the card so that it is the same height as the side walls. Draw a gate in the middle of the strip, as shown, or design your own.

5 Mix up gray paint for the stone walls and paint the sides of the box, inside and out. Use a big brush and splodge on different shades of gray, with little dabs of white and black for a realistic stone effect.

6 Paint the inside of the box a splodgy brown—mix red and yellow with a little blue, to make it look muddy.

7 Remember to paint the end wall and gate, too. Put the box and gate to one side to dry.

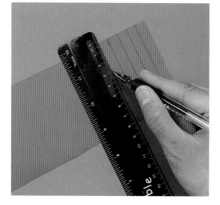

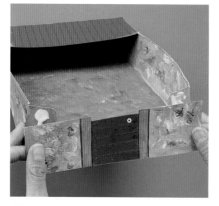

oink

8 Meanwhile, cut a piece of colored paper to cover the roof that measures 3 in. (8 cm) by the width of your cereal box. If you'd like to add the effect of a corrugated roof, draw evenly spaced lines across the width with the fine black pen and a ruler.

9 Use a glue stick or brush a thin, even layer of glue on the roof part of the pigsty, and stick the paper on top. Brush glue on the side flaps and attach the end wall, using paper clips to hold it in place while the glue dries.

10 When the glue is dry, remove the paper clips and add some pigs (see page 50), straw (page 110), and a feeding trough or two (page 112), to make them feel at home!

TIP

You could paint the roof
instead of using paper.
Rub sandpaper on the shiny
card to make it easier to
apply the paint.

Dovecote

A toilet-paper tube is the perfect size for a dovecote, with a couple of perches for resting on, and long legs to give them a good view.

You will need

Toilet-paper tube

Cereal-box card

Colored paper for the roof

White paper

Arch template (see page 126)

A round object, like a cup, about 3 in. (8 cm) diameter

Paper clips

White paint

Paintbrush

Glue stick

Craft scissors

Ruler

Pencil

Black felt-tip or marker pen

1 Paint the toilet-paper tube white and put it to one side to dry. Meanwhile, cut a ½ x 6-in. (1 x 15-cm) strip from the cereal-box card and cut it in half. Put to one side for later.

2 Make the roof from the colored paper. Find something to draw around that's roughly double the diameter of your tube (about 3 in./8 cm), such as a cup. Draw around it on the paper and carefully cut out the circle.

3 Lightly fold the circle in half, only pressing down in the very middle (to avoid heavy fold lines). Lightly fold it in half again, just pressing down on the pointy tip, to get the center of the circle.

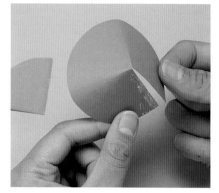

4 Open up the circle and follow the crease lines to cut out a quarter section. Rub glue stick on one edge of the three-quarter circle and fold it to form a cone shape.

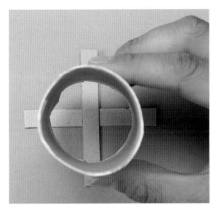

5 Work on your dovecote again when the painted tube is dry. On a flat surface, make a cross with the two strips of card you cut earlier. Make sure the strips are at right angles, and then place the tube over the top. Look down the tube to check the center of the cross is in the center of the tube.

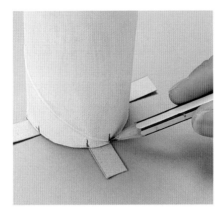

6 Hold the top of the tube steady with your hand, and use a pencil to mark where the edges of the strip touch the tube. You should end up with eight pencil marks.

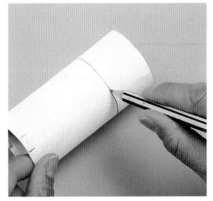

7 About one third of the way down the opposite end, lightly draw a line all the way around the tube. This is only a guide, so don't worry if your line is a bit wobbly!

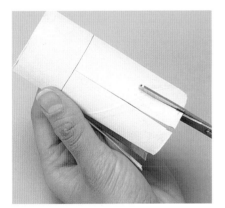

8 Cut straight up from each of the eight pencil marks to the marked line.

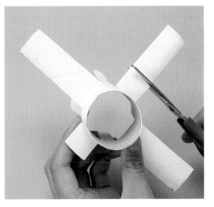

9 Bend back the four wider strips, leaving the thinner ones down for the legs. Cut back the ends of two opposite strips to reduce their length to make perches.

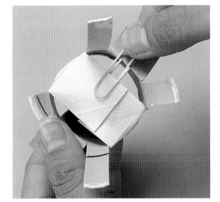

10 Cut back the two remaining wide strips by half and bend them under the dovecote (press firmly along the fold), so they overlap. Trim if you need to, and glue them together. Use a paper clip to hold the strips in place while the glue dries.

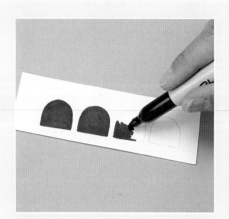

11 Copy the template on page 126 to draw four arched doorways on white paper. Color them in with the black pen and cut out.

12 Apply a little glue stick to the back of the doorways and glue them in place, positioning two of them above the perches. Now set the roof on top, once you've put a dove inside (see page 57)!

Wishing Well

A toothpick makes a clever winch, and the rest of the well is made from just one toilet-paper tube.

You will need

Cereal-box card

Toilet-paper tube

Toothpick (cocktail stick)

Modeling clay (plasticine)

Paper clips

Paint (white, black, red, yellow, and blue)

Paintbrush

Glue

Sticky tape (optional)

Craft scissors

Small scissors (see page 8)

Ruler

Pencil

Fine black felt-tip or gel pen

1 Cut a strip of cereal-box card, about ½ x 3 in. (1 x 8 cm), to help with measuring. Put the toilet-paper tube on top of this strip, so when you look down the tube, the strip is in the center.

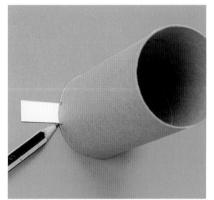

2 With a pencil, mark where the strip edges touch the tube on both sides. You will have four marks.

3 About one third of the way down the opposite end, lightly draw a line all the way around the tube. This is only a guide, so don't worry if your line is a bit wobbly!

4 Cut straight up from the four pencil marks to the marked line.

5 Bend back the thinner strips a little, so you can cut off the wider ones in between, leaving a well base and two upright posts.

6 For the roof, use one of the leftover pieces of toilet-tube card as it already has a curved shape. Shorten it so it's just a little wider than the diameter of the tube. Straighten the front and back edges if necessary.

7 Paint the well with splodges of light and dark gray for a realistic stone effect. Take a brown (mix red, yellow, and a dab of blue) and paint the posts, a toothpick (cocktail stick), and a small strip of spare card (for the winch handle). Paint the well roof a color of your choice. Stick the end of the toothpick in some modeling clay (plasticine) while it dries.

8 When the paint is dry, use a pencil to mark the inside of the posts, about ¾ in. (2 cm) above the well base. Lay the marked card over a piece of modeling clay, and use small scissors to make holes through both posts (keep the scissors closed, press down, and twist from side to side). The holes should be big enough for the toothpick.

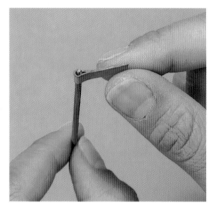

9 Snip the sharp ends off the toothpick, fold the small strip of card in half, and glue it over one end (attach a paper clip to hold it on the toothpick while the glue dries). Trim it shorter, if necessary, when dry.

10 If you like, draw some tiles or shingles on the well roof, using a fine black pen.

11 Fold the top ¾ in. (2 cm) or so of the posts inward, and glue them (or use sticky tape) to the inside top curve of the well roof.

12 When the glue is dry, give the well roof a gentle squeeze to bring the front and back edges down. Push the toothpick into place through the holes that you made in step 8.

chapter 4
machinery & scenery

The tractor chugs along the lane
with a load of hay, it's feeding
time down on the farm, and
dinner's on its way!

Machinery

Every farm needs a tractor and trailer! There are two options: the quicker one with wheels glued on, or the moving wheels option, using brads (paper fasteners). Once you've made the tractor and trailer, you could adapt these ideas to make other farm machinery, such as a plow (plough) or bale lifter.

vroom

vroom

TIP

When cutting around a circle, hold the scissors steady while turning the card slowly toward you as you cut.

Tractor

The tractor is a big project, but not a really complicated one—just lots of steps and plenty of circle-cutting practice! Adult supervision is needed for the hole making.

You will need

Toilet-paper tube (1½–2 in./4–5 cm diameter is best)

Cereal-box card (one large box)

Plain paper

Newspaper

3 circle shapes to draw around (about 2¾ in./7 cm diameter cup, 1½ in./4 cm diameter egg cup, and a large coin, such as a quarter/10 pence)

Front wheel support and lights templates (see page 126)

Craft scissors

Tacky glue (see page 8)

Red, black, white, and yellow paint

Paintbrush

Paper clips

Pencil

Ruler

Black marker pen with a fine/medium nib

Silver metallic pen (optional)

Sandpaper (optional)

For a moving tractor (optional):

Small scissors (see page 8)

4 brads (paper fasteners)

Modeling clay (plasticine)

Gray marker pen

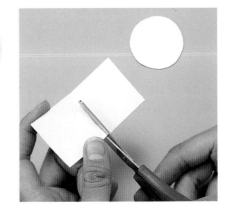

1 Place one end of the toilet-paper tube on some cereal-box card and draw around it with a pencil. Cut out the circle. Use a ruler to draw a 1½ x 3 in. (4 x 8 cm) rectangle on the card (use a corner of the card for one side) and cut this out, too. Fold the rectangle in half and cut along the crease, so you have two matching squares. These will be the back wheel supports.

2 Paint the tube, the two squares, and the circle red (or your chosen tractor color). Paint a small piece of card yellow, for the lights. Put all the pieces to one side to dry.

3 Meanwhile, make the wheels. Find a circle shape, like a cup, with a diameter of about 2¾ in. (7 cm) for the larger back wheels, and a smaller one, with a diameter of about 1½ in. (4 cm), like an egg cup, for the front ones. Draw two big circles and two smaller ones on cereal-box card and cut out carefully.

4 Mix up a gray and paint the center of the wheels—you don't need to go right up to the edges. Put to one side to dry.

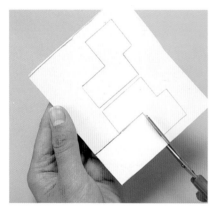

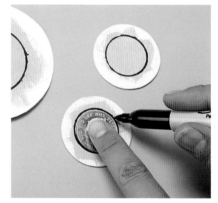

5 Use the template on page 126 to cut out two front wheel supports from card. Make sure they're opposites (flip the template over to draw the opposite shape).

6 Paint the top part of the support (the rectangle) gray, for the engine. When the paint is dry, draw thick black lines with the marker pen. Or, if you have a silver metallic pen, use it to draw around the edge of the engine part and then add thick silver and black stripes down the middle.

7 The center of the wheels should be dry now. Place the medium round object (the egg cup) in the middle of the large back wheel and draw around it with the black marker pen. Draw around it several times to make this black ring nice and thick. Do the same using a large coin in the middle of the smaller front wheels.

8 Either color-in the tires with the marker pen, or finish them with black paint.

9 If you'd like to paint the back of the tires, too, rub the shiny card with a little sandpaper to remove the sheen so that the paint will grip the surface.

10 Cut a 1 x 2-in. (3 x 5-cm) piece of card and paint or color it in black, for a seat.

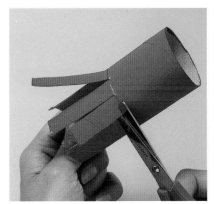

11 To make a steering wheel, draw around the coin on some card and cut out. With a black pen, draw lines crossing through the middle and draw around the edge of the circle.

12 Take the red tube, which should be dry, and at one end make two pencil marks on the edge 1½ in. (4 cm) apart. Then above these marks, about halfway along the tube, lightly draw a line across—don't worry if it's a bit wobbly, the line is just a guide. Cut straight up from both marks to the pencil line.

13 Make another two evenly spaced cuts between the cut sides, up to the line. Don't worry if the three strips aren't exactly the same. Leave the middle one and bend back and snip off the outside two.

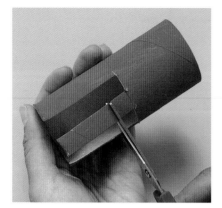

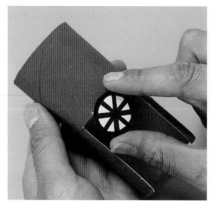

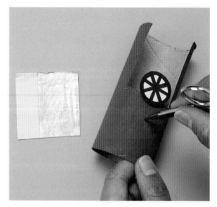

14 Shorten the remaining central strip to about ½ in. (1 cm), to make a tab to attach to the steering wheel.

15 Put a little tacky glue on the tab and stick the steering wheel in place.

16 Cut a 2 × 2 in. (5 × 5 cm) square of plain paper for the funnel and paint or color in about half of it gray or silver. Roll into a tight tube. Use the small scissors to make a hole for the funnel on top of the tractor hood, in line with the steering wheel (keep the scissors closed, press down, and twist from side to side).

TIP
It's really worth using tacky glue (see page 8) for this project—it makes gluing pieces to the cardboard tube much easier.

beep

beep

17 Make sure the hole is big enough for the end of the funnel, and push it into place.

Time to attach the wheel supports

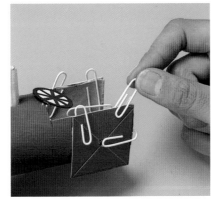

18 Skip this step if you aren't making moving wheels. Take the square back wheel supports that you painted in step 2. To find the center, use a ruler and pencil to draw lines from opposite corners of the square that cross in the middle. Place the center of the square over a piece of modeling clay (plasticine) and make a hole through the center with small scissors. Do the same with the other square.

19 Brush tacky glue on half of each square only, on the back. Line up the gluey part with the back corner and top edge of the driver's cabin. Hold in place with plenty of paper clips!

20 Skip this step if you aren't making moving wheels. For the front wheel supports, find the center of the small square below the engine, by drawing lines from opposite corners that cross in the middle. Place on top of some modeling clay and make a hole through the center of the square with small scissors.

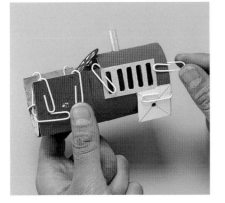

21 Brush tacky glue on the back of the engine part only. Line up the front edge of the small square with the front edge of the tube, and make sure the top edge of the engine part is lined up with the top edge of the driver's cabin. Attach lots of paper clips to hold in place, including a few on the non-glued parts (the front wheel supports), as this helps bend the top part of the card to the curve of the tube.

22 When the glue is dry, take the paper clips off and bend the bottom part of all the wheel supports back into place. Check they look even and gently squeeze the tube back into shape if it needs it.

Wheel time!

23 If you don't have brads (paper fasteners), or want a faster, easier tractor option, then draw on central bolts with the black marker pen and simply stick the wheels onto the wheel supports. Try to keep the squares roughly in the center of the wheels. When you're happy, use paper clips to hold the wheels in place and allow to dry on its side. Go to step 28.

24 If you want moving wheels, draw one back wheel and one front wheel (using your circle shapes to draw around) on some plain paper and cut them out. Fold them carefully in half, then in half again. Unfold them and where the creases cross will give you the center.

25 Place a paper circle on top of a matching wheel, with a piece of modeling clay underneath for safety. Pierce a hole through the center of the paper and the card with small scissors. Repeat for all four wheels. Make sure the holes are a good size—check the brad fits through and the wheels can spin around.

26 Make holes in the tube by pushing the small scissors through the holes in the back wheel supports.

27 Attach the back wheels with brads, opening up the pin on the inside of the tube. Push a brad through the front of a smaller wheel and bend the front wheel support back a little, so you can thread the pin through the hole and open it up. Repeat for the other front wheel.

Finishing touches

28 Take the red circle for the tractor front that you painted in step 2 and use a ruler and black marker pen to draw a line across the top. Draw lines straight down from each end and join at the bottom to make a square or rectangle.

29 For the front radiator grill, draw thick black lines with the marker pen. You can color in between the lines with a silver or gray pen, if you like.

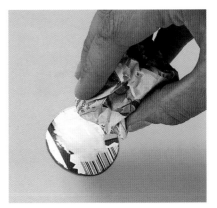

30 Scrunch up a piece of newspaper (about 8 x 6 in./ 20 x 15 cm) and glue it onto the back of the tractor front.

31 When the glue is holding, brush more glue around the inside edge of the tractor tube and push the newspaper end into the tube, tucking in any bits as you go, until the card circle is level with the front of the tube.

32 Draw two circles on the yellow painted card for lights—either draw them free-hand or use the template on page 126. Cut out carefully and glue near the top of the tractor front.

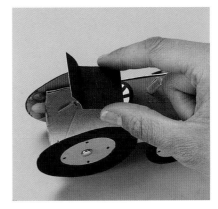

33 Bend the black card seat that you made in step 10 in half, and glue inside the driver's cabin at the bottom of the tube. Leave a space at the back for attaching the trailer.

Trailer

Like the tractor on page 99, you can make the trailer with moving wheels if you like. Adult supervision is needed for the hole making.

You will need

Small cardboard box (such as a teabag box)

Cereal-box card (5 x 5 in./ 12 x 12 cm)

Colored paper

Tow bar template (see page 126)

2 circle shapes to draw around (about 1½ in./4 cm diameter egg cup and a large coin, such as a quarter/10 pence)

Craft scissors

Glue

Black and white paint

Paintbrush

Paper clips

Ruler

Pencil

Black marker pen with a fine/ medium nib

Fine black felt-tip or gel pen

For a moving trailer (optional):

Plain paper

Small scissors (see page 8)

2 brads (paper fasteners)

Modeling clay (plasticine)

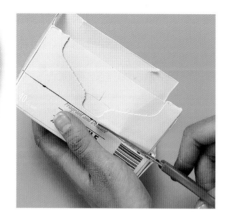

1 Use the black marker pen and ruler to measure and mark 1½ in. (3 cm) up from the base of the box on all sides. Join the marks and cut along the line.

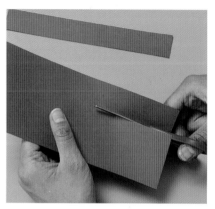

2 Cut 1½-in. (3-cm) wide strips from the sheet of colored paper. Cut right along the whole length of the sheet. You may need two or more strips to wrap around the box.

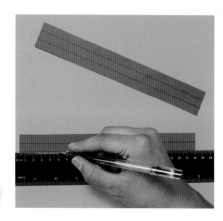

3 Use a ruler and the fine black pen to draw two evenly spaced lines at ½ in. (1 cm) intervals along the length of the paper strips.

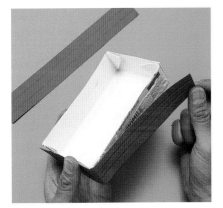

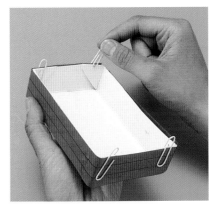

4 Brush a thin, even layer of glue on two sides of the cardboard trailer (a short end and long side) and carefully press a paper strip into place, taking extra care around the corners.

5 Brush glue on the remaining sides, and keep working round, overlapping the ends of the first strip with the new one.

6 When you've wrapped the strip right around the box, cut away any extra paper, leaving a little to overlap, and glue in place. You may find there are flaps of card inside the box base. Glue these down and use paper clips to hold them in place while the glue dries.

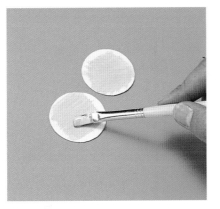

7 The two wheels should be the same size as the front wheels of the tractor, so if you have made the tractor, use the same circle shape. Draw around it twice on some card and cut the circles out.

8 Mix a gray and paint the center part of the wheels—you don't need to go right up to the edges. Put to one side to dry.

9 Meanwhile, copy the template on page 126 and cut out the tow bar from card. Paint or color in if you like. Brush glue on the rectangular part only, and stick it under one short end of the trailer, centered in the middle.

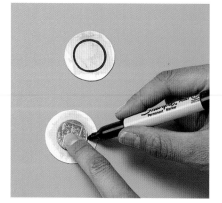

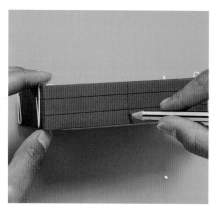

10 The center of the wheels should be dry now. Place the coin in the middle of the painted wheel and draw around it with the black marker pen. Draw around it several times to make this black ring nice and thick.

11 Either color in the tires with the marker pen, or finish them with black paint. Add bolts to the gray center.

12 About halfway along the trailer sides, draw a light pencil line down to the base—don't worry if it's a bit wobbly, the line is just a guide.

14 To make moving wheels, cut another wheel circle from some plain paper. Fold it in half, then in half again. Unfold the circle and where the creases cross will give you the center.

13 If you don't have brads (paper fasteners) or want a faster, easier trailer option, glue the wheels on the sides so the top of the wheel is just below the top of the trailer. Use the pencil lines as a guide to center the wheels. Leave the trailer on its side to dry and go to step 18.

15 Place the paper circle on top of a card wheel, with a piece of modeling clay (plasticine) underneath for safety. Pierce a hole through the middle of the paper and the card with small scissors (keep them closed, press down, and twist from side to side). Do the same for the other wheel. Make sure the holes are a good size—check the brad fits through and the wheels can spin around.

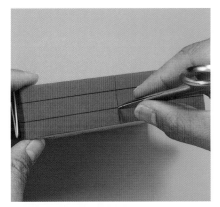

16 On the trailer, use the small scissors to make a hole where the pencil line crosses the bottom pen line, on both sides.

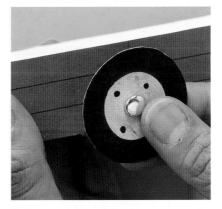

17 Attach the wheels with the brads, pushing them through the holes in the wheel and the trailer, and opening on the inside of the box.

18 Join two paper clips together and clip one end to the trailer's tow bar and the other to the back of the tractor.

tweet, tweet

Hay Bales & Stacks

You will need

3 sheets of tissue paper (2 yellow, 1 orange)

Small card box, like a bouillon (stock) cube box (about 2¼ in./6 cm long)

Yogurt pot

Glue

Long scissors

Craft scissors

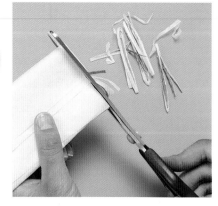

1 First, loosely fold the sheets of tissue paper together, so you can easily cut across the width with one snip of your long scissors. Keep the strips as thin as you can.

2 Unfurl the strips and tear or cut them up until you have a good quantity of different lengths of yellow and orange strands.

3 For the bale, you'll need a small card box. Brush glue on one end and press it into the tissue paper strands. Press and pat down with your hand. Repeat at the other end.

4 Do the same on all the sides, one at a time, taking care to press the tissue paper strands around the edges.

5 You'll probably have a rather wild looking hay bale by now! Press, pat, and gently squeeze as you turn it in your hands. Trim any stray strands, but leave a few for a natural look.

6 For the haystack, use a small yogurt pot with curved sides. Brush glue on the base and press it into the pile of tissue paper strands. Pat and press down with your hand.

7 Brush some glue on a section of the side, and press a small handful of tissue paper into the glue. Pat and press down with the palm of your hand and your fingers. Work around the pot.

8 Cut away any long, stray strands and cut off the rim of the yogurt pot, if you want. This is best done by an adult, as the plastic is hard to cut.

Trough

You will need

Toilet-paper tube

Craft scissors

Glue

Paint

Paintbrush

Ruler

Pencil

Paper clips

Dried couscous (optional)

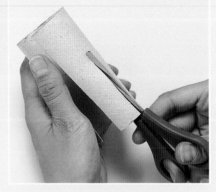

1 Cut a strip from the length of the tube, about 1 in. (2 cm) wide.

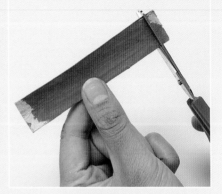

2 You can either leave the trough plain or paint both sides of the strip. You don't need to paint right up to the ends. When the paint is dry, trim away the unpainted ends to neaten it up. If you've left yours plain, shorten the strip by about 1 in. (2 cm).

3 Fold the strip in half lengthwise, to make it more trough shaped.

4 For the leg supports, unfold the card strip and draw a pencil line about ½ in. (1 cm) in from each end. Carefully snip down both sides of a pencil line, almost to the fold, but not across it. Do the same at the other end. The pieces should still be attached in the middle. If you cut the legs off by mistake, don't worry— just have another go.

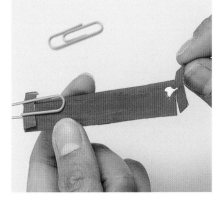

5 On the back of the trough, dot a little glue in the middle, near the join. Bend the legs right back and attach to the trough with paper clips to hold them in place.

6 When the glue has dried, remove the paper clips and bend the legs down. Trim them if you need to, so the trough stands level.

7 Dried couscous makes good animal feed for the trough, or see what else you can find.

oink

Scenery

Set the scene for your farm with a few trees, some grass to graze, and a pond for the ducks to paddle in. If you'd like to make a base for all the different pieces, then try using large sheets of green or brown paper for fields for your animals. You could cut a piece of gray or brown paper to make a farmyard base, and cut a lane for the tractor to drive along. Arrange hedges or walls by your farm.

Pond

A sheet of blue paper is all you'll need to create a tranquil pond for the ducks, with the option of grass or reeds too.

You will need

Blue paper or cereal-box card and blue paint

Craft scissors

Green paper (optional)

Glue stick (optional)

1 Cut a pond shape from blue paper, or use cereal-box card and paint it blue.

2 To add some grass or reeds around the edge, cut a strip of green paper about 1½ in. (4 cm) wide. Fold the bottom third lengthwise. On the wider part, snip zigzags along the length, but don't cut across the fold. Make your stems of grass different heights and widths.

3 If you would like the grass strip to curve around the shape of the pond, make a few snips below the grass, up to the fold. This will make it easier to attach and glue beneath the pond.

4 Apply glue stick on the back of the pond, along the edge where you want the grass, and glue the snipped edge in place.

Grass & Flowers

You will need

Green paper

Colored tissue paper

Craft scissors

Glue

1 For tufts of short grass or grass for grazing, cut a strip of green paper, whatever length you want and about ¾ in. (2 cm) wide. Fold in half lengthwise. For taller grass, cut a wider strip and fold the bottom third lengthwise.

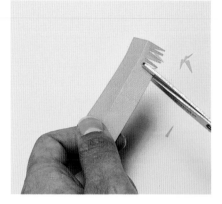

2 On one side, snip zigzags along the length, but don't cut across the fold. Make your tufts of grass different heights and widths.

TIP

To cut several squares of tissue paper in one go, fold a sheet of tissue paper a few times before you cut.

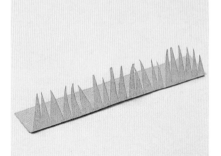

3 Press along the fold again so that the grass stands upright, and position your grass tufts where you want them to grow.

4 For the flowers, cut small squares of tissue paper then scrunch and roll them up into little balls. Glue the flowers in your fields by some grass.

Stone Walls

You will need

Cereal box

Glue

Black and white paint

Big paintbrush

Sandpaper (optional)

Long scissors

Craft scissors

Ruler

Pencil

Paper clips

Colored felt-tip pens

1 First, open up a cereal box and cut away the flaps and the side seam to leave you with a large rectangle of card. Then, use a ruler and pencil to draw as many 2½-in. (6-cm) wide strips as you can along the length of the card.

2 Cut out the strips and then cut a gentle, uneven wave along one edge for the top of the stone wall.

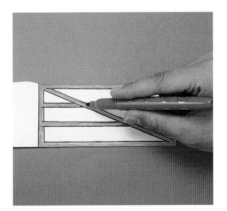

3 At the end of one of your strips, draw a gate—design your own or follow the picture. Make it about 5 in. (13 cm) long and cut a thin strip off, along the top, so the gate is a little shorter than the wall. Color it in with felt-tip pens. Fold the card where the gate meets the wall, so the gate opens.

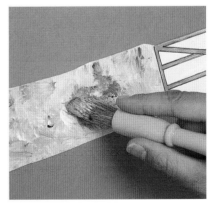

4 Mix plenty of white paint with a small amount of black and use a big brush to paint light and dark gray splodges along the card strips. Use a few dabs of white and black for a realistic stone effect.

5 If you want to paint the shiny side of the card too, rub sandpaper over it first, to remove the sheen, so the paint goes on more easily.

6 Glue a few sections together, overlapping each piece a little and attaching paper clips top and bottom to hold in place. The more sections, the bigger your enclosure.

7 When the glue is dry, remove the paper clips and arrange the wall using the original cereal packet folds to make it stand. Add extra folds if you like, to change the shape.

Hedge

The hedge is made the same way as the stone walls, but uses strands of tissue paper, similar to the hay bales, for a natural effect.

You will need

3 sheets of green tissue paper
(1 light green if possible)

Cereal box

Glue

Long scissors

Craft scissors

Ruler

Pencil

Paper clips

Colored felt-tip pens

1 First, loosely fold the sheets of tissue paper together, so you can easily cut across the width with one snip of your long scissors. Keep the strips as thin as you can. Unfurl the strips and tear or cut them until you have a good quantity of green strands.

2 Next, open up a cereal box and cut away the flaps and the side seam to leave you with a large rectangle of card. Then, use a ruler and pencil to draw as many 2½-in. (6-cm) wide strips as you can along the length of the card. Cut them out.

moo

3 At the end of one of your strips, draw a gate—design your own or follow the picture. Make it about 5 in. (13 cm) long and cut a thin strip off, along the top, so the gate is a little shorter than the hedge. Color it in with felt-tip pens. Fold the card where the gate meets the hedge, so the gate opens.

4 Brush a good layer of glue along the card strip, leaving a glue-free gap about ½ in. (1 cm) wide at one end. Press a small handful of tissue paper strands into the glue and work along the card. Do both sides if you want and repeat for all the strips. Put something heavy, such as a few books, on top of the strips while the glue dries.

5 When the glue is dry, trim the top and bottom of your hedge strips.

6 Brush glue on the hedge-free ends and stick sections together. The more sections, the bigger your field. Attach paper clips top and bottom to hold the glued ends in place.

7 When the glue is dry, remove the paper clips and arrange the hedge using the original cereal packet folds to make it stand. Add extra folds if you like, to change the shape.

snort

Tree

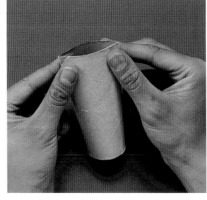

1 For the trunk, take the tube and pinch the sides together at one end to make crease lines near the top.

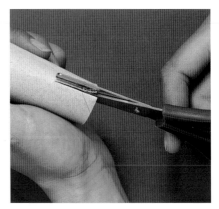

2 Cut down each crease by about ¾ in. (2 cm). Make sure each cut is the same length. Snip out an extra sliver of card to widen the slots.

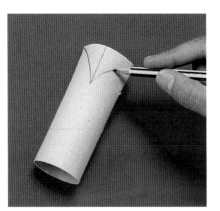

3 About halfway between the two slots, draw a pencil line down from the edge of the tube to just below the end of the slots. Draw a curved line from the top of each slot to the bottom of the pencil line, to form the branches.

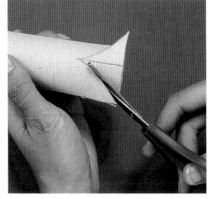

4 Cut along the curved lines to remove this section.

5 For the top of the tree, either copy and cut out the template on page 126 from cereal-box card, or draw your own tree top. If drawing your own, make sure the base has a straight line in the middle. This needs to be about the width of your tube.

6 Push the center section of the tree top into the trunk slots. When you're happy it looks even on both sides, use a pencil to mark where the tree top slots into the trunk.

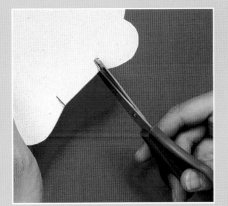

7 Take the tree top out and make small cuts on the marked lines, about ½ in. (1 cm) long, and cut out an extra sliver to widen the slots slightly, as before. Check the tree top fits into the trunk.

8 Separate the top and the trunk and paint them. Make a brown from yellow mixed with red and a dab of blue, and, if you don't have green paint, mix blue with yellow to get the perfect leafy shade.

9 When the paint is dry, reassemble the tree and add it to your farm to provide some shade for the sheep (see page 12), or a roost for Bluebird and Robin (see page 28).

Templates

Some of the projects have templates to copy. There are a few different ways to use the templates: either copy freehand, trace them, or photocopy them. This last option is probably the best. Use a glue stick to glue a photocopied page on to a similar-sized piece of cereal-box cardboard and leave to dry under something heavy, like a pile of books. Roughly cut out the templates first, then neaten up each shape. Remember to label them, and keep them somewhere safe, so you can always make more. To speed things up, have a go at copying some of the small, simple-shaped templates freehand.

All templates are printed at 100%, so there is no need to enlarge them!

Dog (page 38)

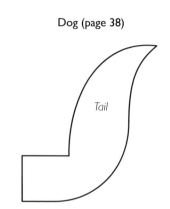

Tail

Sheep (page 12)

Head

Owl (page 33)

Head

Tail

Dog and Fox paw

Pig (page 50)

Head

Cat (page 54)

Head

Fox (page 31)

Tail

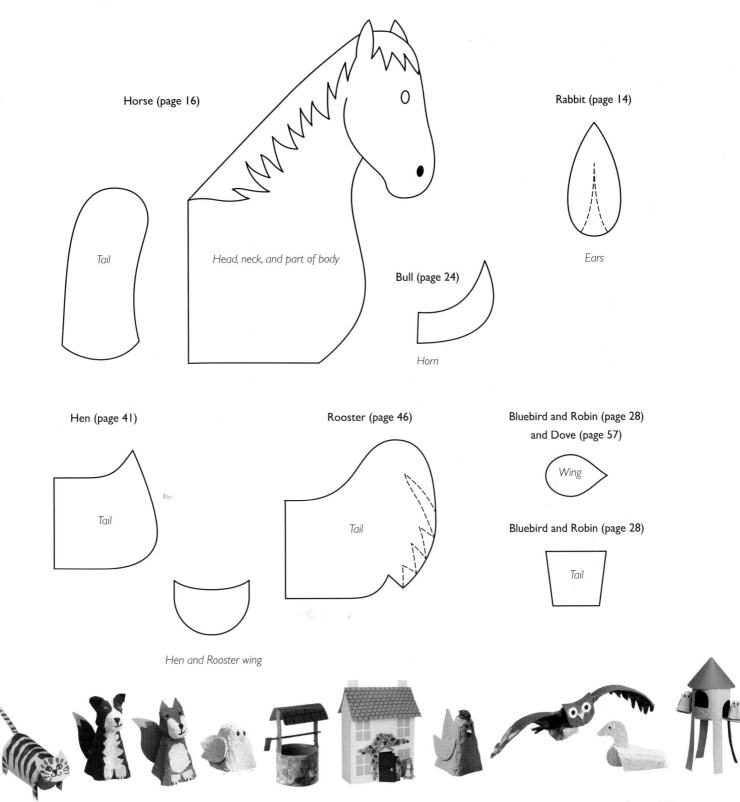

Horse (page 16)

Tail

Head, neck, and part of body

Bull (page 24)

Horn

Rabbit (page 14)

Ears

Hen (page 41)

Tail

Rooster (page 46)

Tail

Bluebird and Robin (page 28)
and Dove (page 57)

Wing

Bluebird and Robin (page 28)

Tail

Hen and Rooster wing

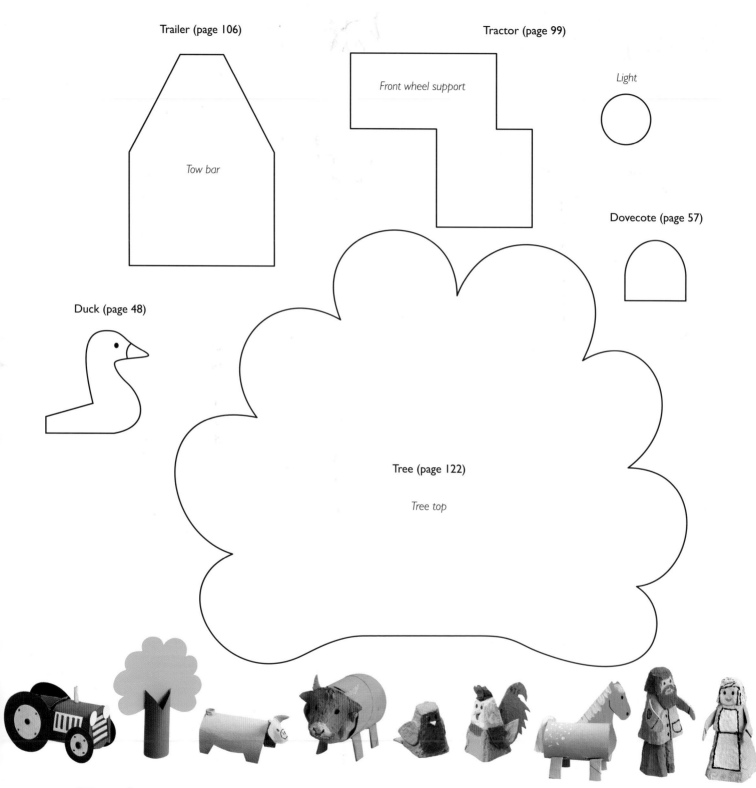

Trailer (page 106)

Tow bar

Tractor (page 99)

Front wheel support

Light

Dovecote (page 57)

Duck (page 48)

Tree (page 122)

Tree top

126 templates